INDIAN VEGETARIAN COOKBOOK

Prava Majumder
Sumita Sen-Gupta

Times Books International
Singapore • Kuala Lumpur

Cover Photography by Yim Chee Peng
Inside Photography by Yim Chee Peng
except pages 2, 21 and 22 by Andrew Merewether

© **1989 Times Books International**
Times Centre, 1 New Industrial Road
Singapore 1953
2nd Floor, Wisma Hong Leong Yamaha
50 Jalan Penchala
46050 Petaling Jaya
Selangor Darul Ehsan
Malaysia

All rights reserved. No part of this pubication
may be reproduced, stored in a retrieval system, or
transmitted, in any form or by any means,
electronic, mechanical, photocopying, recording or
otherwise without the prior permission of
the copyright owner.

Printed by Times Offset Pte Ltd
ISBN 9971 65 301 X

CONTENTS

Message from Dr Hena Mukherjee	v
Indian Cuisine – how it all began	vi, vii
Vegetarian Cooking	viii
Classes of Food	ix, x
Weights and Measures	xi
Spices	2, 3, 4, 5

Cereals and Grains	6, 7
Cereals and Grains and their Nutrient Contents	8
Butter Rice	28
Coconut Milk Rice	23
Flour Vatura	16
Indian Stuffed Bread	18
Loochi	21
Milk Poori	15
Navaratnam Pilau	30, 31
Paratha stuffed with peas	12
Plain Khichri	24
Plain White Rice	22
Potato Paratha	17
Roghni Naan	20
Radish Paratha	11
Sour Yogurt Chapati	10
Vegetable Fried Rice	25
Vegetable Pilau	26
Yogurt Kulcha	19
Wholemeal Chapati	9

Roots and Tubers	32, 33
Roots and Tubers and their Nutrient Contents	34
Dry Potato Tarkari	35
Potato Dom	39
Potato Kima Curry	41
Potato Mattar Rasa	37
Potato with Spinach	36
Steamed Potato Dum	40
Yam Dalna	43

Yellow Vegetables, Gourds and Squashes	44, 45
Yellow Vegetables and their Nutrient Contents	46
Bitter Gourd Vaji	48
Carrot Tarkari	52
Drumstick Curry	47
Long Watery Pumpkin	49
Sweet Pumpkin Chokka	51
White Radish Tarkari	53

CONTENTS

Green Vegetables and Vegetable Fruit	54, 55
Green Vegetables and their Nutrient Contents	56
Bati Chorano	57
Cabbage Dalna	65
Cabbage Dom	64
Cabbage Tarkari	73
Cauliflower and Mushroom	59
Cauliflower Korma with Garnish	60
Cauliflower with Coconut	58
Eggplant Baratha	67
Eggplant Dolma	71
Eggplant Puree	66
French Beans and Mushroom Bhaji	68
French Beans with Coconut	69
Fried Beans	72
Mixed Vegetables	74
Mixed Vegetables with Coconut	75
Panir Devil Curry	63
Unripe Fruit	76, 77
Unripe Fruit and their Nutrient Contents	78
Green Banana Kopta	79
Mixed Fruit Chutney	83
Unripe Papaya Curry	81
Unripe Jackfruit Curry	80
Legumes and Lentils	84, 85
Legumes and Lentils and their Nutrient Contents	86
Chana Dhall	92
Dhall Sambar	88
Green Split Peas Dhall	87
Horse Gram Dhall Kopta Curry	90
Mysore Dhall	93
Vegetable Dhall	92
Savouries	94 – 107
Pickles and Chutneys	108 – 115
Desserts and Sweet Drinks	116 – 120
Guide to Picking the Freshest Vegetables	122 – 125

A Message *from Dr Hena Mukherjee*

As world awareness swings towards physical fitness and healthier living styles, more people are taking a fresh look at their food habits and are beginning to appreciate a diet that taps on the bounties of nature.

In ancient Indian literature, one reads of ascetics who lived on only herbs and vegetables and presumably remained healthy for many decades! Present-day vegetarian communities prove this to be a fact. There seems to be less illness among them and they are very rarely plagued by the physical problems meat-eating societies face.

Like the Chinese, traditional Indians classify vegetables under "cooling" and "heat-producing" categories. "Cooling" vegetables are found in almost the whole range of gourds and squashes considered by many to be stodgy and unwholesome. For example, the bitter gourd – though its seeds are used in medicinal preparations and its fruit is a well-known source of Vitamin C – is often shunned. But piquantly-spiced and mixed with other complementing vegetables, it is said to help us cope with hot weather.

In cooler climes, we need to turn to vegetables that are seen as energizers. These can easily be found in carrots, tomatoes and a whole range of green leafy vegetables. This category is also a source of carotene or Vitamin A, essential in maintaining one's eyesight; it also helps build an immunity to infection and aids bone development.

It is also to be expected that, in our new awareness of nutrients, we be concerned about our intake of carbohydrates, which many of us tend to consume more than we really need. Besides flour, cereals and sugars, vegetables and fruits are included in this category, but their caloric value is lower, and therefore healthier.

In Asia, there is an exotic range of vegetables which, when cooked with suitable herbs and spices, can often produce meals more exciting to the palate than non-vegetarian ones. And, individually or as an accompaniment, they provide the essential difference that can make a gourmet meal out of an ordinary dish.

Vegetables, cooked Indian-style, are often flavoured with herbs and spices. And many ingredients, apart from adding that extra dash of flavour, possess medicinal properties as well. The popularity of garlic pearls as a nutritional supplement today bears testimony to the ancient Indian folk belief that garlic helps the athritic and rheumatic, besides being able to control cholesterol levels.

Herbs, such as mint and fennel, are the leaves of plants, which, over the centuries, have been found to be useful for both culinary and health reasons. Spices, which are the seeds, roots and fruits of plants, are generally more aromatic and stronger-flavoured than herbs. And that elusive flavour and teasing aroma found in Indian cooking can often be traced to a fascinating mixture of spices, each blend changing the taste of the dish fundamentally. Spices are often associated with pungent flavours, such as peppers, but there are also sweet, aromatic flavours like cinnamon, cardamom and cloves, the "garam masala" that the writer uses in many of her dishes.

We can say that whoever is involved in the selection and preparation of food decisively influences the health and happiness of her beneficiaries or "victims" as the case may be! This book is dedicated, therefore, to all of us who yearn for healthier and happier lives. – **Dr Hena Mukherjee**

Indian Cuisine – *How it all began*

Indian cuisine is a rich heritage handed down over the years, a story of its history and geography and of its various religions. And it stands for subtlety and sublimity in flavour and taste.

Many of India's eating and cooking habits can be traced directly to its geography, and North and South (with some deviations along the coastline) are its main cooking divisions. Another influence has been its rich history, with dietary restrictions emerging from the main religion of the sub-continent, namely Hindu.

The differences between North India and South India are many. In North India, various groups of conquerors took over the country, influenced its culture and left their mark on its cuisine, which still finds echoes in recipes today.

Generally speaking, Northern Indian cuisine is not one of necessity, but of sumptuousness – having evolved in the royal courts – and rich with spices, herbs and sauces. The Moghuls, in particular, bore a strong influence and so too the Persians, with their fondness for rice-based dishes. (Many of the famous Indian pillaus are Persian in character, if not in origin.)

In South India, there is less evidence of external influences because the mountains of the south and its treacherous terrain were a hindrance to would-be invaders. As a result, the South Indians tend to be more orthodox Hindus than the North Indians.

Not all Hindus are vegetarian but Hinduism does demand an abstinence from meat at least once a week. Most South Indian Hindus follow a vegetarian diet and the higher their caste, the more closely they adhere to the stricter aspects of the faith. (The Brahmana or priest caste, for example, exclude even eggs from their diet.)

In North India, dietary customs of the Hindus tend to be interpreted more leniently. The only meat forbidden is beef, from the sacred cow.

The belief in sacred animals stemmed from the pre-Aryan cultures of Mohenjaro-Daro and Harappa. Animal worship was practised and the bull, especially, was considered sacred. Killing one was taboo and it was believed that the deed could lead to the ruin of a harvest or result in major calamities like floods and disease.

Yet, it is interesting to note that Hindus were, for a time, a meat-eating people. For thousands of years, Hindus were under the influence of sacrificial cults, a practice brought in by the Aryan invaders in 1,500 B.C. During this period, the Hindus were extremely unprejudiced in their diet, eating the meat of fish, horse, cattle, sheep and even dogs. As part of religious ceremonies, animal sacrifices replaced earlier offerings of foods such as milk, ghee, grain and the intoxicating liquor known as soma, and meat became an integral part of the Hindu diet.

Hundreds of years passed before the Age of Buddha. During this period was spread such beliefs as reincarnation (samsara) and karma, the fundamental laws of cause and effect. Buddhism did not expressly forbid the eating of meat but discouraged the killing of animals. But in the 12th Century, when the Hindu king Asoka converted to Buddhism, vegetarianism became a precept of Buddhism. And even meat-eating Hindu priests, who had earlier been performing animal sacrifices, turned vegetarian. Not everyone followed *a vegetarian diet and those in the lower castes, for example the kshatriya or warrior castes, chose to remain meat-eaters.*

Jainism, another of India's ancient religions, also had a profound influence. Its followers, known as Jains, go by an extremely strict moral code of which ahimsa (non-violence) forms an integral part. To kill animals is forbidden and, in fact, strict Jains wear masks to prevent breathing on live organisms.

The end of the 17th Century was the phase in which the modern development of Hinduism began, brought about by a number of reformers. At this time, too, there was more contact with the West through European invaders like the Portuguese. This phase saw the works of great philosophers and theologians who contributed an enormous amount of religious literature.

By the 19th and 20th Centuries, Hindu beliefs had been altered considerably, at least in the cities and among literate people, because of changing social conditions and the influence of Western ideas. But its principles of non-violence and respect for all living things still remain.

Today, food is divided by the Hindus into three categories – satvik, rajsik and tamsik. Sages and old people follow the satvik vegetarian diet, which is intended to provide peace of mind; all foods which contain spices and excite the senses are forbidden. Rajsik – like satvik – is essentially vegetarian, but includes onions, garlic and various spices, as well as light wine; it is intended for the average family. The third – tamsik – is a diet meant for the kshatriyas (warriors) and the lowest caste. In this diet, liqour and meats are permitted.

What makes Indian vegetarian cuisine so unique is its subtle blend of spices, mixed in such a way that they form the integral flavour of the dish. And the real challenge of Indian cooking lies in obtaining just the "right" combination of the many spices. This combination, or "masala", has components that are carefully measured. Yet it combines so well with the other spices in the dish that none predominates.

Even the way in which Indian food is served is unique. In the South, meals are often served on banana leaves; elsewhere, each diner has his own thali, a round tray in which are placed individual bowls of the food being served.

It is customary to eat with fingers of the right hand, the left being considered unclean. Styles vary, with North Indians using only the tips of their fingers while South Indians tuck in, more or less, with the whole hand.

Vegetarian Cooking – *The Way to Healthy Eating*

Vegetarians, as the name implies, do not eat fish, fowl or meat. But do you know there are divisions of vegetarians as well? Those who follow the "lactarian" diet include dairy products in their meals. With the "ovo-lactarian" diet, eggs are a further addition, and the "vegan" diet is one that excludes all forms of animal products.

A question frequently asked is: Does a vegetarian face nutritional deficiencies? It all depends on the kind of vegetarian you are or intend to be. Following a "lactarian" or "ovo-lactarian" diet can be nutritionally adequate but "vegans" run the risk of being nutritionally deficient by not having a well-balanced diet.

What exactly is a well-balanced diet? Both vegetarians and non-vegetarians need the same amount of nutrients for a nutritious well-balanced diet, which should, normally, consist of 20% protein, 50% carbohydrate and 30% fat, as well as vitamins and minerals.

Eggs, meat, fish and milk are high-quality proteins and are considered "complete" proteins. The quality or completeness of a protein refers to the essential amino acid composition of the food; it must contain all the essential amino acids in the proper proportions. Proteins obtained from vegetables are considered less complete since they are lack at least one or two of the essential amino acids.

Those who follow either the lactarian or ovo-lactarian diets do not face nutritional deficiencies. Vegans, on the other hand, run the risk of an inadequate intake of Vitamin B12 and calcium, both of which are derived from animal products.

It is interesting to not that in a study, it was found that vegetarians were between 15 and 20 lbs lighter in weight than non-vegetarians. Vegetarians enjoy other advantages; they generally have a much lower blood pressure than non-vegetarians and also a better cholesterol profile.

In discussing any diet, energy requirements have to be considered. Each person has a varying energy demand, depending on such factors such as his weight, sex, age and the amount of activity he does. A healthy man requires between 1600 and 1800 kcal daily.

CARBOHYDRATES

Carbohydrates are the least expensive food sources of heat and energy, and the most readily available. Basically, they fall into three categories: starches, sugars and fibre. Starches are present in the cereals (such as wheat, rice, maize, oats, rye, millet and sorghum), the pulses (such as peas and beans), the tubers (such as potatoes), and green vegetables. Sugars are found in sugar, honey and syrup as well as fruits. Fibre is found in fruits, vegetables, grains and pulses. The best sources of carbohydrates are plant foods – fresh fruits and vegetables, and whole grains.

There is nothing wrong in having a carbohydrate-rich diet, if proteins and fats are included in the diet. But if you are overweight, it is wise to limit its intake because, consumed in excess, they turn into fat and are stored as fat deposits.

FATS

Fats are a concentrated food source of heat and energy and are essential to health because they fulfil specific biochemical functions. Yet it is too much fats, and the wrong kinds, that make for poor nutrition.

Fats should contribute up to 30 % of the calories in the diet and, preferably, be unsaturated rather than saturated. Saturated fats, for example, butter, cream and cheese are of animal origin, while unsaturated fats, like the corn and soya bean oils, are of plant origin.

In addition to obvious fats like butter, margarine and lard, the other foods that contain fats are milk, fatty fish, eggs, nuts, grains, seed and fruits such as olives and avocadoes.

With a higher standard of living, there is a greater tendency to take too much fats, and at the expense of carbohydrates and protein. And it has proved that too much fats in the diet contributes to a higher incidence of heart problems and degenerative diseases.

To remain healthy, therefore, it is wise to limit your intake of fats, especially those of the saturated kind.

PROTEIN

Protein is made up of amino acids and we need it to build new cells and to repair tissues.

We obtain protein directly, by eating plant foods, or indirectly, by eating the flesh, milk and eggs of animals who feed on plants.

Protein-rich foods from animal sources are said to be complete proteins in that they supply all the amino acids necessary in our diet. Vegetable protein is said to be incomplete because they supply only varying amounts of the essential amino acids that are of nutritional value. So the way to achieve an effective and complete vegetable protein is to combine vegetables containing different amino acids that complement each other.

Combined correctly, vegetable protein can be superior to meat protein since animal fats are absent and there is more fibre content to help rid the body of toxins.

VITAMINS, MINERALS... AND WATER

Vitamins and minerals are essential for growth, tissue repair and regulating metabolism. Present in all three of the food categories mentioned – carbohydrates, fats and proteins – they are needed only in small quantities.

While carbohydrates, fats, protein, vitamins and minerals all contribute, in their own way, to a healthy and well-balanced diet, we must not forget water, that other indispensable. The body needs between six and eight glasses a day to function well.

Utensils used in Indian cooking

Indian cooking is exotic but it can be done in ordinary equipment.
Here are some of the more popular utensils and their substitutes:
The Karhai – a wide pan with a curved base. Used for frying foods like potato dum. Substitute with the more commonly-known wok or any deep frying pan.
The Tawa – a circular iron disc which is very slightly concave. Used as a griddle for frying various types of bread. Substitute with a heavy iron frying pan.
The Granite Mortar and Pestle. Used for grinding ingredients such as dry spices and chillies. Gives off a unique aroma when done this way and no serious cook of Indian cooking should be without one. An electric blender is considered by many to be a poor substitute.
The Pressure Cooker. Though a Western utensil, it is a boon to the Indian cook. Used very effectively in the cooking of dhall as it cuts cooking time and less water is required.

WEIGHTS AND MEASURES

A cook in India hardly uses standard measurements. She takes a pinch of this and a sprinkling of that and goes by taste to decide whether the dish has just the right flavour.

If you have never had the opportunity to observe or cook in an Indian kitchen however, you would need to follw the exact amounts as given in the recipes.

As you gain more experience, you will adjust the amounts accordingly, for example using less salt or adding more chilli powder. But it would be wise not to adjust the amounts of spices since it is the combination of these spices that give the dish its distinctive flavour.

The teacup is referred to simply as the cup in all the recipes. The cup is used as a standard measure and it is approximately two-thirds of a metric cup. Given below are the cup measurements and their equivalents in both Metric and Imperial measures.

METRIC	IMPERIAL
¼ cup = 60 ml	¼ cup = 2 fl oz
½ cup = 125 ml	½ cup = 4 fl oz
¾ cup = 185 ml	¾ cup = 6 fl oz
1 cup = 250 ml = ¼ litre	1 cup = 8 fl oz = ½ pint (US)

Use either Imperial or Metric measure, but not a mixture of both since the metric cup is approximately 10% greater than the Imperial cup.

Below is a list of Mass weight measures and their equivalents:

IMPERIAL	METRIC
15 g	½ oz
30 g	1 oz
60 g	2 oz
90 g	3 oz
125 g	4 oz
185 g	6 oz
250 g	8 oz
375 g	12 oz
(1 lb) 500 g	16 oz

Top Plate: (clockwise)
Ginger, Almonds, Clove, Star Anise, Turmeric, Dry Chilli, Cardamom, Bay Leaves, Cinnamon Sticks
Bottom Plate: (clockwise)
Sweet Cummin, Kunyit Powder, Fenugreek, Cummin Seed Powder, Small Cummin Seeds, Mustard Seeds, Coriander Seeds, Chilli Powder

> This section gives information on the spices and other ingredients used in this book.

Asafoetida:
More popularly known as hing in Indian spice stores.

Basmati:
Also known as Patna rice. A special long-grain Indian rice. Can be subtituted with any good-quality rice.

Bay leaves:
Used mostly in its dried form, to flavour curries and rice dishes.

Cardamom:
There are two types: brown and green. The larger and more pungent brown cardamom is used to flavour savoury food; the green looks almost white, due to the bleaching process it goes through, and is used to flavour both savoury and sweet dishes. Cardamom can be used whole (in pods) or in powder form. When grinding cardamom to powder, discard the pod and use only the seeds inside.

Chillies:
The chilli is an essential ingredient in Indian cooking. There are two types of fresh chillies. The longer, slightly less hot variety is 10 – 15 cm in length. The smaller variety is only about 1 cm long but very hot! Fresh chillies are red or green. Dried in the sun, they take on a brownish-red colour. Dried chillies can either be used whole or ground to make chilli powder.

To mildly flavour a dish while cooking, simply wash chilli and add it at simmering stage. Discard the chilli just before serving. Indian cooks prefer to leave the chilli in the dish. To prepare chilli, slit lengthwise, remove seeds and discard stalk. (You can remove seeds by scraping them out with the tip of a small, sharp knife. Wear gloves if you are not used to handling chillies. Otherwise, make sure you wash hands thoroughly after the process – chilli stings!) Alternatively, cut the chilli into two, lengthwise, removing central membrane and seeds. The seeds of dried chillies are easy to remove; just cut and shake to dislodge seeds.

Since it is the seeds of a chilli that make it potent, leave them in when you want a dish hot and discard if you prefer it less hot.

Cinnamon:
One of the most popular spices, since it can be used for savoury as well as sweet dishes. Cinnamon can be bought either in stick or powder (ground) form, which tends to be less flavourful when stored for too long. Cassia is a spice similar to cinnamon, but its flavour is not as delicate nor as aromatic. To distinguish the two, look out for the thickness of each stick. Cinnamon sticks are much thinner and smoother, unlike the cassia which has a corky layer.

Cloves:
Cloves have a strong aroma and flavour. It is sometimes used as an analgesic to soothe toothache and its oil is used in perfumes. Cloves should be used sparingly in cooking to enhance the flavour of certain dishes.

Coriander seeds:
Coriander seeds have been used in the East for hundreds of years. They give a fresh lively zest to vegetables and lentils. Dried coriander seeds are beige in colour. They have to be roasted (not fried) before they are crushed or ground. Coriander leaves can be used to flavour curry.

Coconut milk:
To make fresh coconut milk, add 3 cups warm water to 2 cups grated coconut. Mix well, squeeze and strain. If fresh coconut is not available, add boiling water to desiccated coconut and strain through a fine cloth, like muslin. Remainder milk can be stored in a feeezer.

Cummin:
An essential ingredient in most curries as they are aromatic and peppery. There are several types of cummin, including black, yellow and light brown. Cummin seeds are roasted before being ground into powder. The best way to roast them is in a frying pan or oven, for four minutes, after which they should give off a strong, spicy fragrance.

Curd:
Plain yogurt. Can be made by stirring 1 teaspoon yogurt into a cup of slightly warmed milk and then set aside, covered, for 3 – 4 hours. Store in refrigerator till it turns hard. Process can be repeated for other lots of yogurt.

Curry leaves:
Curry leaves are often used in South Indian cooking. They are small and dark green in colour, with toothed edges. Distinctly aromatic, they add flavour to curries. In India, curry leaves are so plentiful that they are used fresh. Elsewhere, the dried leaves are more common. When using dried curry leaves, soak them in a little water first before adding them to the dish.

Dhall:
Also known as lentils, dhall is widely used in Indian cooking. Gram Dhall or Chana Dhall is the largest type of lentils; mysore dhall are small, red lentils; moong dhall are green split peas; urhad dhall are black split peas. To prepare dhall, fry in a pan without oil and then wash and boil.

Fennel:
Spicy seeds. Fennel looks a little like cummin but are more whitish in colour. Because of its appearance, sweet fragrance and flavour, it is also known as sweet cummin. It can be bought in its powdered form. Aniseed, though quite different, is often used as a substitute.

Fenugreek:
Fenugreek seeds are small, flat and squarish, and brownish-beige in colour. They are used in curries both for flavouring and for thickening. Fenugreek is slightly bitter in taste so it should be used sparingly, never exceeding the amount stated in the recipe. The seeds should be roasted just long enough to release their aroma; too much and they will taste even more bitter.

Garam masala:
A mixture of ground cinnamon, cardamom and cloves in these proportions: 4 tablespoons cinnamon, 2 tablespoons cardamoms and 1 tablespoon cloves. Dry mixture in the sun before grinding into powder if preferred.

Garlic:
Garlic, an ingredient very often used to enhance the taste of food, has, for many generations, also been known for its medicinal properties. In India, it has been used as an antiseptic lotion to wash wounds and ulcers; the ancient Egyptians used it to treat ailments such as heart problems, headaches and tumours.

The cream-coloured garlic bulb is divided into sections known as cloves, which are held together by a film of thin skin. This skin is always peeled before use.

Ghee:
Also known as butteroil, ghee is what gives North Indian cooking its distinctive flavour. It is actually clarified butter or pure butter fat and can be bought in cans or packets. It is useful in cooking because, having no milk solids, it can be heated at much higher temperatures without burning (unlike butter). You can make your own ghee: Heat unsalted butter till it melts and froths. Spoon off froth from the top and pour the melted butter into a heatproof glass bowl. Leave to cool. Strain through fine muslin to remove any residue. Will keep 3-4 months without refrigeration. If you want the flavour of ghee without the cholesterol, just add 1 teaspoon of it to the cooking oil just before cooking.

Ginger root:
An important ingredient in Indian cooking and often used in folk medicine to cure colds and stomach ache. The root is knobbly and light cream in colour. To use it, scrape off the thin skin and then either chop, grate, slice or grind to a pulp. If fresh ginger is unobtainable, substitute with powdered ginger. Use 1 teaspoon for every 4 cm length of ginger.

Ginger juice:
Made by adding a little cold water to pounded ginger and then squeezing for juice. If fresh ginger is not available, add just enough water to powdered ginger for a thick consistency.

Khoa:
An ingredient used in Indian sweetmeats. To make, very gently simmer cow's milk over low fire till it comes to the boil. Stir till milk becomes a thick consistency. Five cups will yield 5 oz.

Madras curry:
A typically South Indian taste. The majority of the curries in this book are North Indian. If you prefer South Indian flavours, it is quite easy to alter these recipes to suit your taste. Simply add curry leaves, tamarind or lemon juice, a larger amount of hot spices and substitute coconut milk for yogurt.

Milk:
Thin milk mentioned in the recipes refers to fresh milk, not the powdered variety. Thick milk mentioned refers to unsweetened, evaporated milk. If

fresh milk is used in the cooking of panir (see notes below), there is no need to use ghee. However if powdered milk is used, then a little ghee should be added in the kneading stage.

Mint leaves:
Although there are many varieties, the common round-leafed species is the one most often used in cooking. Mint adds flavour to curries and chutneys.

Mustard powder:
You can buy mustard powder ready-prepared or make your own. Dry, or roast whole mustard seeds till they crackle, then grind and use as specified.

Mustard seeds:
There are three varieties of mustard seeds – black, reddish-brown and white. The mustard seeds used in Indian cooking are usually of the black variety. To obtain the full flavour of the seeds, they should be fried quickly in very hot oil.

Nutmeg:
An important ingredient in curries. Nutmeg comes from a species of tree native to the Moluccas. When ripe, the fruit splits, exposing the dark brown nut – the nutmeg we are familiar with. The fragrance and flavour of the nutmeg is stronger when it is grated finely just before use.

Oil:
Any vegetable oil may be used in the recipes. However, in the making of pickles, use either mustard oil or olive oil.

Onion juice:
See directions on how to obtain ginger juice.

Panch masala:
The mixture of five spices in these proportions: 2 tablespoons black cummin seeds, 2 tablespoons sweet cummin seeds, 2 tablespoons cummin seeds, 1 tablespoon fenugreek and 2 tablespoons mustard seeds. Panch masala is used in some vegetable curries and chutneys.

Panir:
Home-made cream cheese. To make, use 6 cups milk. Bring milk to the boil, stirring occasionally to prevent top from thickening. As the milk starts to rise to the surface, pour in a mixture of 2 tablespoons vinegar and 6 cups cold water. Stir slowly till milk curdles. Set aside for 5 minutes to cool and then strain through fine muslin cloth; wash under running water and then hang cloth bag up till all water has drained away. Panir is also known as chana.

Pepper, black:
Pepper enhances the flavour of a dish; it also aids digestion. It is always better to use freshlyground black pepper because pepper loses its fragrance very quickly once it is made into powder form.

Roasted cummin seeds:
Can be bought. To make your own, heat cummin seeds in a frying pan or oven for a few minutes till they turn slightly brown and give off a strong spicy fragrance. Roasted cummin seeds can also be ground into a powder when required.

Sesame seeds:
Tiny, almond-shaped seeds that are creamy-white in colour. They add a nutty flavour to a dish.

Shallots:
Small purplish onions with reddish-brown skin. They grow in clusters and resemble garlic cloves in shape.

Syrup:
Made by boiling sugar and water. Use proportions as required in individual dessert recipes.

Tamarind:
This piquant-tasting fruit is shaped like a large broad bean and has a brittle brown shell. Inside the shell are shiny dark seeds covered with dark brown flesh. The tamarind fruit is dried and sold in packets. When recipe calls for tamarind juice, soak seeds in ½ cup cold water, squeeze and strain. Substitute with lemon juice if unavailable.

Turmeric:
A rhizome of the ginger family. Turmeric has an orange-yellow colouring which is a mainstay of commercial curry powders. Though it is often referred to as Indian saffron, the two should not be confused and should never be used interchangeably.

Yeast:
Also known by its Indian name khamir. To make yeast, mix 1 tablespoon plain flour and ½ cup yogurt. Set aside for 2 – 3 days to ferment.

Cereals and Grains

CEREALS AND GRAINS

Like bread in the West, rice forms the basis of an Indian meal, and the preparation of it has been developed to a fine art – from simple boiled white to elaborate and highly-spiced biryanis.

Many different varieties of rice grain are used: polished, unpolished, long-grained, short, even rice that has been matured over many years. Each variety has a different method of preparation and several methods are featured in this section.

The cooking of rice is an art. Rice that is cooked to perfection should have each grain separate; well-done right through, firm, fluffy and neither too soft nor too hard. Bread is also an important item in the Indian diet, the most popular being the chapati. Flat and unleavened, it hardly resembles Western-style bread though it does bear a likeness to the Mexican tortilla.

There are many variations of the chapati. The thick, coarse variety is called roti while the refined ones, light and thin in texture, are known as chapatis. Then there are the pooris – deep-fried, puffed-up and light in texture, and parathas – heavier, shallow-fried and can either be left plain or stuffed. Whatever variation, all are served piping hot. And the skill of a cook depends on how the texture of each of these breads turns out!

All Indian dishes, except the sweet desserts and some of the savouries, are eaten with either rice or bread, but never together.

Cereals and Grains and their Nutrient Contents

Calories	★ ★ ★ ★
Protein	★
Fat	—
Calcium	★ ★
Iron	★ ★ ★
Vitamin A	—
Vitamin B Complex	★ ★ ★ ★
Vitamin C	—
Fibre	★ ★ ★ ★ ★

None	—	Fair	★ ★ ★
Negligible	★	Good	★ ★ ★ ★
Some	★ ★	Very Good	★ ★ ★ ★ ★

WHOLEMEAL CHAPATI (North India)

Makes: 12　　*Preparation: 15 minutes*　　***Cooking Time: 20 minutes***
　　　　　　Kcal/portion: 111　　***Leavening: 30 minutes***

Ingredients:

- 3　cups wholemeal flour
- ½　teaspoon salt
- 1　tablespoon corn oil or ghee
- 1　cup warm water

Method:

Sift the flour, add salt and, using fingers, rub in the corn oil or ghee.

Add the warm water gradually and knead mixture to form a soft dough.

Wrap dough with a piece of muslin or soft kitchen towel and set aside for ½ hour.

Remove muslin and divide dough into 12 equal portions.

Dust each portion with flour and roll into a thin, flat pancake about 5 in (12.5 cm) in diameter.

Heat a frying pan or tawa till it is medium hot.

Place one pancake in tawa and press down gently, using a piece of cloth or soft towel.

When chapati rises, turn it over and press it down. When chapati puffs up, remove from pan and place in a deep bowl, covered. Repeat with remaining portions. If you wish, you can dab a bit of ghee on to each chapati while it is still hot.

Serve chapati hot, with Potato Dom.

CEREALS AND GRAINS

SOUR YOGURT CHAPATI (North India)

Makes: 12   Preparation: 10 minutes   Cooking Time: 20 minutes
Kcal/portion: 117   Leavening: 30 minutes

Ingredients:

- 3 cups wholemeal flour
- ½ teaspoon salt
- ½ cup sour yogurt
- A little warm water
- 1 tablespoon corn oil or ghee

Method:

Mix wholemeal flour with the salt, yogurt and warm water. Knead mixture to form a soft dough.

Cover dough and set it aside for 30 minutes.

Rub corn oil (or ghee) into dough before dividing it into 12 equal portions.

Shape each portion into a ball and dust with a little flour.

Roll each portion into a thin, flat pancake about 5 in (12.5 cm) in diameter and 2 mm thick.

Heat a griddle. When hot, fry each chapati, turning it over many times till it puffs up. Keep heat on low.

When chapati is done, remove from pan and allow to cool.

Store cooled chapatis in a container with a tight-fitting lid.

Serve Yogurt Chapati with any vegetable curry.

CEREALS AND GRAINS

RADISH PARATHA (Gujerat)

Radish Paratha tastes delicious even when eaten on its own.

Makes: 12   *Preparation: ½ hour*   *Cooking Time: ½ hour*
Kcal/portion: 309

Ingredients:

- 2 lb (1 kg) white radish or carrot
- 2 teaspoons salt
- 1 cup ghee or corn oil
- 1 teaspoon black cummin seeds
- 2 teaspoons sugar
- 2 teaspoons chilli powder
- 2 cups plain flour
- 1 cup wholemeal flour
- 2 tablespoons warm water

Method:

Wash and peel radish (or carrot). Grate finely, mixing a little salt to taste; squeeze and discard juice.

Heat 1 tablespoon oil and add black cummin seeds. When mixture starts spluttering, add radish (or carrot), 1 teaspoon sugar, and chilli powder. Fry for about 15 minutes before removing from heat.

Using fingers, mix the two types of flour, 1 teaspoon salt and the remaining 1 teaspoon sugar with 2 tablespoons slightly heated ghee. Add warm water and knead flour well, adding more water (if necessary) to form a soft dough.

Divide dough into 12 equal portions.

Shape each portion into a ball and make a dent in the centre. Place some cooked mixture in the dent and close up to cover filling. Roll each filled paratha into a flat, circular shape.

Heat a tawa or frying pan and fry each paratha on medium heat, using 3 teaspoons oil. Turn paratha over many times till it puffs up and is slightly brown on both sides.

Remove from heat. Repeat with other portions.

Serve Radish Paratha hot with any chutney.

CEREALS AND GRAINS

PARATHA STUFFED WITH PEAS (Bihar)

Makes: 12   Preparation: ½ hour   Cooking Time: ½ hour
Kcal/portion: 299

Ingredients:

1   cup corn oil
1   tablespoon melted ghee
1   onion, chopped
1   cup fresh green peas
1½ teaspoons salt
1   teaspoon sugar
2   teaspoons chilli powder
½   teaspoon pounded ginger
½   cup cold water
½   teaspoon garam masala
3   cups plain flour

Method:

Put 3 teaspoons oil into heated frying pan. Add chopped onion and fry till brown.

Add peas, 1 teaspoon salt, the sugar, chilli powder, pounded ginger and a little cold water (from the ½ teacup).

Cook mixture till it turns dry.

Add garam masala to pea mixture just before removing from heat. Mash and set aside.

Mix flour with 1 tablespoon melted ghee (or corn oil) and the remaining ½ teaspoon salt.

Knead the flour mixture with fingers, adding just enough cold water to make a very dry soft dough. Divide into 12 portions.

Shape each portion into a ball and, using a bit of oil, roll out into a flat circular pancake about 2 mm thick.

Place a bit of the cooled pea mixture in the centre of each pancake. Fold it into two, dust with a little flour and press edges down to seal, as in a curry puff.

Heat a tawa or frying pan. Fry parathas separately, using about 3 teaspoons oil for each one. Turn paratha over many times till it puffs up and turns slightly brown. Remove from pan and repeat with remaining portions.

Serve parathas with any chutney or vegetable curry.

CEREALS AND GRAINS

Paratha Stuffed with Peas

CEREALS AND GRAINS

14

Milk Poori

CEREALS AND GRAINS

MILK POORI (South India)

Makes: 20   Preparation: ½ hour   Cooking Time: ½ hour
             Kcal/portion: 164

Ingredients:

- 2   cups plain flour
- ½   cup wholemeal flour
- 1   teaspoon salt
- 1   teaspoon sugar
        Ghee or oil for deep frying
- ½   cup thick coconut milk or unsweetened milk★

Method:

Mix both types of flour with the salt, sugar and 2 tablespoons melted ghee or cooking oil. Rub in thoroughly, then add the milk slowly, kneading well to make a soft, dry dough. Add a little cold water if necessary.

Divide the dough into 20 equal portions and form small balls. Using a little oil, roll each ball into a flat circular shape about 1 mm thick.

Heat ghee (or oil) for deep-frying. When hot, fry pooris separately. Turn each poori over a few times till it puffs up and is light brown. Remove and drain well.

Serve with any vegetable curry.

★ *Squeeze one teacup grated coconut with one teacup warm water, then strain for milk.*

CEREALS AND GRAINS

FLOUR VATURA (Punjab)

Flour Vatura is a kind of sour dough bread. It looks like a big poori and can be a very filling meal eaten with Sour Kabli Chana or Potato Curry.

Makes: 12 *Preparation: ½ hour* *Cooking Time: ½ hour*
Kcal/portion: 199 *Leavening: 4 hours*

Ingredients:

- 3 cups plain flour
- 1 teaspoon salt
- 2 teaspoons sugar
- 1 teaspoon bicarbonate of soda
- 2 cups ghee or oil
- 6 teaspoons soaked yeast
- 1 cup semolina soaked in water for about 5 hours

Method:

Mix flour with the salt, sugar, semolina, bicarbonate of soda and 1 tablespoon melted ghee (or oil). Rub in well and then add the yeast and water, a little at a time, till it forms a soft, dry dough. Knead well. Cover and set aside for four hours.

When dough has risen, apply 2 teaspoons ghee (or oil) to fingers and knead till it becomes soft and pliable.

Divide dough into 12 equal portions and form small balls; roll out into flat circular shapes about 4 in (10 cm) in diameter. Dust each pancake with a little flour before placing them on a tray. Cover with a damp kitchen towel.

Fry each pancake in hot oil. Turn it over many times till golden brown and puffed up. Remove from heat and drain well.

POTATO PARATHA (North India)

Potato Paratha can be a complete meal in itself. It is also delicious eaten with chutney.

Makes: 10   **Preparation:** ½ hour   **Cooking Time:** ¾ hour

Kcal/portion: 337

Ingredients:

- 2 cups cooking oil
- 2 teaspoons shredded ginger
- 1 large onion, *chopped*
- 4 medium-size potatoes, *mashed*
- 3 teaspoons salt
- 1 teaspoon sugar
- 2 teaspoons chilli powder
- 2 teaspoons fried cummin seed powder
- A few coriander leaves, *chopped*
- 1 teaspoon garam masala
- 4 cups plain flour
- 1 cup wholemeal flour

Method:

Heat 1 tablespoon oil on medium heat and fry the ginger and onion till light brown. Add the mashed potato, a little salt, sugar, chilli powder, fried cummin seed powder and coriander leaves. Fry till mixture turns soft, then add garam masala. Mix well and remove from heat.

Mix both types of flour with a bit of salt and 2 tablespoons cooking oil. Rub in well till it becomes a soft, dry dough. Add water if necessary.

Divide the dough into 10 equal portions.

Using a little oil, roll out each portion into a flat, circular shape.

Spread a little of the potato mixture in the centre of a paratha and then roll out another paratha over it. Press edges tightly to seal and roll again lightly.

Rub a little oil onto a heated griddle and fry 'double paratha' one at a time. Turn over and fry until light brown, adding a little more oil if necessary. Remove from heat.

Serve with chutney.

CEREALS AND GRAINS

INDIAN STUFFED BREAD

Makes: 12   Preparation: ½ hour   Cooking Time: ½ hour   Soaking of dhall: Overnight
Kcal/serve: 235

Ingredients:

- 1 cup black split peas dhall
- 2 cups ghee or oil
- 2 teaspoons asafoetida powder *
- 2 teaspoons chilli powder
- 1 teaspoon sugar
- 2 teaspoons salt
- 2 teaspoons sweet cummin powder, *roasted*
- 2 cups plain flour
- ½ cup wholemeal flour
- 2 teaspoons baking powder

Method:

Soak the dhall overnight.

Wash and grind dhall coarsely, using a little water.

Fry the ground dhall with 1 tablespoon melted ghee (or oil). Add the asafoetida powder and fry till light brown. Add chilli powder, sugar, salt and roasted cummin seed powder. Fry for about ten minutes, then remove from heat.

Mix both types of flour together. Add 1 teaspoon salt, baking powder and 1 tablespoon melted ghee. Rub in thoroughly, then add water slowly to make a soft dry dough.

Divide dough into 12 portions.

Stuff a little cooked dhall mixture in the centre of each ball and then close up.

Roll each ball into a circular, flat shape and dust with a little flour.

Heat ghee (or oil) for deep-frying. Fry each portion separately till it puffs up and turns golden brown. Remove and drain.

Serve with chutney.

* *If asafoetida powder is not available, substitute with 2 onions, finely chopped.*

CEREALS AND GRAINS

YOGURT KULCHA OR DEEP FRIED BREAD (Gujerat)

Makes: 12 *Preparation: ½ hour   Cooking Time: ½ hour*
Kcal/portion: 170   Leavening: 4-5 hours

Ingredients:

- 2 cups plain flour
- ½ teaspoon salt
- 1 teaspoon sugar
- 1 teaspoon baking powder
- 3 tablespoons beaten yogurt
- 1 cup ghee or oil for frying

Method:

Mix flour with the salt, sugar, baking powder, yogurt and a little warm water. Knead for a bit, then keep it covered for about 4 or 5 hours.

When flour has risen, add 4 teaspoons melted ghee (or oil). Knead till dough is soft and dry.

Divide dough into 12 portions. Roll out each portion into a flat, circular pancake, using a little ghee (or oil).

Fry each pancake in ghee (or oil) on medium heat. When pancake puffs up and turns slightly brown, remove and drain well.

Serve Yogurt Kulcha with any chutney or Potato Curry.

CEREALS AND GRAINS

ROGHNI NAAN (North India)

Naan are traditionally baked in a clay oven called a tandoori. If you do not own one, the baking method used in this recipe is just as effective.

Makes: 8   *Preparation: 20 minutes   Cooking Time: 10 minutes*
Kcal/portion: 228   Leavening: 4-5 hours

Ingredients:

- 1 oz (30 g) fresh yeast
- ½ cup warm unsweetened milk
- 4 teaspoons sugar
- 3 cups plain flour
- 2 tablespoons beaten yogurt
- 2 teaspoons salt
- 2 teaspoons sodium bicarbonate
- 1 tablespoon ghee or butter
- 2 teaspoons black cummin seeds
- 12 almonds, *skinned and chopped finely*

Method:

Soak the yeast with the warm milk and 2 teaspoons sugar. Let stand for a few minutes till it rises and ferments.

Mix flour with the yogurt, salt, sodium bicarbonate and the remaining 2 teapoons sugar.

Add the fermented yeast and knead well, adding a little ghee. Add enough warm water to make a dry dough which will roll out easily. Wrap flour mixture in a tea towel and leave it in a warm place for four or five hours.

After flour mixture has risen, divide into 8 portions. Shape each portion into a ball and then roll out into a thick pancake. Dust with a little flour.

Spread some black cummin seeds and almond bits on top of each pancake (naan).

Set oven at 400° F (205° C). Place naan in a greased baking tray and bake for approximately 10 minutes.

When naan puff up and turn light brown, remove from baking tray.

Serve immediately with a curry or chutney.

LOOCHI (North India)

Makes: 30   Preparation: 20 minutes   Cooking Time: 10 minutes
              Kcal/serve: 130

Ingredients:

1   lb (455 g) plain white flour
¼   lb (125 g) wholewheat flour
½   lb (225 g) ghee
1   teaspoon salt
1   teaspoon castor sugar
1½ cups cold water

Method:

Put both kinds of flour in a mixing bowl. Rub in 4 teaspoons melted ghee, salt and sugar. Make a well in the centre of the flour mixture and add 1 cup water.

Work flour into this well and knead till dough is quite dry. After kneading for about 10 minutes, add 1 tablespoon ghee. Knead again to make a soft dough. Divide the dough into egg-sized lumps and roll out into thin round shapees on a lightly-floured surface.

Heat the remaining ghee in a pan; fry loochis, one at a time, over mediumn heat. Press loochi down with a perforated spoon until it begins to rise.

When it has risen, turn it over and fry till light golden.

Drain well and serve hot with honey, butter or a meat curry.

Loochi

PLAIN WHITE RICE

Serves: 10 Preparation: 5 minutes Cooking Time: 20 minutes
Kcal/serve: 200

Ingredients:

3   teacups rice

Method:

Wash rice thoroughly and then place in rice cooker. Add water till level is 1 inch (2.5 cm) above rice.

When rice is cooked, turn over grains with a fork.

CEREALS AND GRAINS

COCONUT MILK RICE (Kerala)

Serves: 10   Preparation: 10 minutes   Cooking Time: ½ hour
Kcal/serve: 270   Soaking of Rice: 1 hour

Ingredients:

- 2 cups long grain or Patna rice
- 2 cups white grated coconut
- 2 teaspoons salt
- 1 teaspoon turmeric powder
- ¼ cup ghee
- 3 onions, *chopped*
- 2 teaspoons chopped ginger
- ½ cup green peas
- 2 tablespoons raisins
- 20 cashewnuts, *fried*
- 6 fresh red chillies

Method:

Soak rice for 1 hour. Drain and discard water.

Soak the grated coconut in 2 cups warm water and squeeze for milk. Strain.

Place rice in pot or rice cooker. Add salt, turmeric powder and coconut milk. If necessary, add hot water so that liquid level is 1 in (2.5 cm) above the level of rice. Cover pot and cook on medium heat, stirring rice frequently. When three-quarters of the liquid is absorbed, reduce heat to low.

Fry onions and ginger with the ghee till golden brown. Remove and set aside.

When all the liquid in the rice is absorbed, add peas, raisins, cashewnuts, chillies, fried onions and ginger. Mix well and remove from heat.

CEREALS AND GRAINS

PLAIN KHICHRI (North India)

Khichri is a complete meal in itself and easily digested.

Serves: 10   Preparation: 10 minutes   Cooking Time: 30 minutes
Kcal/serve: 411

Ingredients:

- 1 cup long grain or Basmati rice
- ½ cup red Mysore dhall
- 1 cup green split pea dhall (moong dhall)
- ½ teacup ghee or oil
- 4 dried red chillies
- 2 teaspoons chopped ginger
- 2 large onions, *chopped*
- 3 teaspoons salt
- 2 teaspoons sugar
- 2 teaspooons chilli powder
- 2 teaspoons turmeric powder
- 4 bay leaves
- 12 shallots
- 1 teaspoon garam masala
- 4 fresh chillies
- 6 tomatoes, *halved and then sliced*

Method:

Wash rice and both types of dhall. Drain.

Heat the ghee (or oil) in a large pan and fry dried chillies till dark brown. Add ginger and onions and fry till brown.

Add rice, both types of dhall, salt, sugar, chilli powder, turmeric powder and bay leaves. Fry till rice turns a little crispy.

Pour in 9 cups water and cover pan. Cook on medium heat and stir frequently till rice is cooked. (It should be of a soft porridge consistency.)

Add shallots, garam masala and fresh chillies and cook for a further 10 minutes. Add tomatoes just before removing from heat.

CEREALS AND GRAINS

VEGETABLE FRIED RICE (Bengal)

Serves: 10   Preparation: 10 minutes   Cooking Time: ½ hour
Kcal/serve: 301

Ingredients:

- 2 cups long grain or Basmati rice
- 4 florets cauliflower
- 2 carrots
- 3 medium size potatoes
- ½ cup oil
- 3 teaspoons salt
- 1 large onion, *chopped*
- 2 teaspoons shredded ginger
- 2 teaspoons soya sauce
- 4 fresh green chillies, *chopped*
- 1 teaspoon sugar
- ½ cup green peas
- 2 mushrooms, *sliced*
- 2 tablespoons cashewnuts, *fried and ground or pounded coarsely*

Method:

Wash rice and drain rice.

Wash cauliflower, carrots and potatoes and cut them into cubes. Fry vegetables with a little oil and 1 teaspoon salt till slightly brown.

Boil rice with 8 cups water and 1 teaspoon salt. (If using a saucepan, cook with pan covered on medium heat, stirring occasionally.)

When rice is three-quarters cooked, drain all the water and spread rice out on a large tray to cool, separating the grains so that they do not stick together.

Heat the rest of the oil on medium heat and fry onion and ginger till light brown.

Add the boiled rice, soya sauce, green chillies and sugar. Fry for 10 minutes. Put in the fried vegetables, green peas, mushrooms and fried cashewnuts and fry for a further 5 minutes. Remove.

Serve Vegetable Fried Rice with chutney.

VEGETABLE PILAU (North India)

Serves: 6   Preparation: ½ hour   Cooking Time: ½ hour
            Kcal/serve: 430

Ingredients:

- 2 cups long grain or Basmati rice
- ½ cup diced cauliflower
- ½ cup diced carrots
- ½ cup diced French beans
- ½ cup ghee
- 4 sticks cinnamon, each approx. 1 in (2.5 cm) long
- 4 bay leaves
- 5 fresh red chillies
- 5 cardamoms
- 2 teaspoons sugar
- 2 teaspoons pounded ginger
- 1 teaspoon turmeric powder or 1 drop orange food colouring
- ½ cup unsweetened evaporated milk
- 2 teaspoons salt
- ½ cup green peas

Method:

Wash and drain rice.

Wash and drain all vegetables.

In a pan, heat ghee on medium heat and fry cinnamon, bay leaves, chillies and cardamons till they splutter.

Add the rice, sugar, pounded ginger and turmeric powder. Fry till ingredients turn light brown and rice is crispy.

Transfer to a pot or rice cooker. Add evaporated milk and enough water so that liquid is 1 in (2.5 cm) above level of rice. (If using a saucepan, cook on medium heat, stirring rice occasionally.)

In the same pan, fry all vegetables with a little ghee, on medium heat. Add salt.

When vegetables turn slightly brown, remove from pan and set aside.

Check rice. When water is three-quarters absorbed, add the fried vegetables and green peas. Continue to cook over very low heat till all the water has been absorbed.

Remove from heat and serve Vegetable Pilau with any curry or chutney.

CEREALS AND GRAINS

Vegetable Pilau

CEREALS AND GRAINS

BUTTER RICE (North India)

Serves: 10   Preparation: 10 minutes   Cooking Time: 30 minutes
Kcal/serve: 358

Ingredients:

3   cups long grain or Basmati rice
½   cup melted ghee or butter
4   sticks cinnamon, each approx. 1 in (2.5 cm) long
6   cardamoms
8   cloves
2   nutmegs, *pounded finely*
2   teaspoons salt
1   teaspoon sugar
6   bay leaves
1   drop yellow food colouring
½   cup unsweetened evaporated milk
1   tablespoon almonds, *skinned and chopped*
1   tablespoon raisins
10   small onions, *left whole*
1   teaspoon finely chopped ginger
6   tomatoes, *sliced*
5   fresh red chillies

Method:

Wash and drain rice.

Heat ghee. Fry cinnamon, cardamoms and cloves till seeds pop. Add rice, nutmeg, salt, sugar, bay leaves and colouring. Fry till rice turns slightly brown and crispy.

Place rice mixture in rice cooker. Add the milk and sufficient water so that liquid level is 1 in (2.5 cm) above level of rice. (If using a saucepan, cook on medium heat, stirring occasionally, till three-quarters of the liquid is evaporated, then turn heat to low.)

Fry the almonds, raisins, small whole onions and ginger till crispy. Add to rice.

When rice is cooked (all liquid should be completely evaporated), remove from fire.

Place rice on large serving plate and decorate with halved tomatoes and sliced chillies.

Butter Rice

CEREALS AND GRAINS

NAVARATNAM PILAU (Bengal)

Navaratnam Pilau is one of the more elaborate Indian rice dishes and can be served on its own or with chutney.

Serves: 10   **Preparation:** *¾ hour*   **Cooking Time:** *½ hour*
Kcal/serve: *561*

Ingredients:

- 3 cups long grain or Basmati rice
- 3 teaspoons salt
- 3 teaspoons sugar
- 1 cup ghee
- 1 drop yellow food colouring
- 20 cashew nuts, *roasted*
- 2 tablespoons raisins
- 15 almonds, *chopped*
- 2 carrots, *diced*
- 4 florets cauliflower, *diced*
- 1 cup panir cubes
- 4 sticks cinnamon, each approx. 1 in (2.5 cm) long
- 6 cardamoms, *peeled*
- 2 teaspoons shredded ginger
- 4 bay leaves
- 2 seeds nutmeg, *pounded very finely*
- 2 onions, *chopped*
- 1 cup evaporated milk
- Yakhni water (See recipe)
- ½ cup green peas
- 5 fresh red chillies, *sliced*
- 4 tomatoes, *sliced*

CEREALS AND GRAINS

Recipe for Yakhni Water:

Ingredients:

1   piece ginger, approx. 2 in (5 cm) long
1   tablespoon chana dhall or horse gram dhall, *peeled*
1   tablespoon sweet cummin seeds
1   tablespoon coriander seeds
6   dried red chillies
2   sticks cinnamon
6   cardamoms
4   bay leaves

Method:

Wash all ingredients and boil in a saucepan with 12 teacups water. Simmer on very low heat till liquid is reduced by three-quarters. Keep aside to cool, then squeeze and strain through muslin.

Note: It takes only 15 minutes to boil yakhni water if you're using a pressure cooker.

Method:

Wash and drain rice. Mix with salt, sugar, 1 tablespoon ghee (from the one cup) and food colouring. Set aside.

Heat the rest of the ghee on medium heat and fry cashew nuts, raisins and almonds till light brown. Remove.

In the same pan, fry carrot, cauliflower and panir cubes till light brown. Remove.

Now fry the cinnamon, cardamoms, ginger, bay leaves, nutmeg and onions till light brown. Add the rice and fry till it turns a little crispy.

Transfer rice mixture to a pot or rice cooker. Then add milk and sufficient yakhni water so that liquid level is 2 inches (5 cm) above the level of the rice. Cover pot and leave rice to cook. (Stir occasionally if you are cooking it in a saucepan.)

When three-quarters of the water is absorbed, add the fried vegetables, panir cubes, peas and sliced chillies. Cover the pot and keep on very low heat till rice is cooked, adding water, if necessary. Add tomatoes. Remove.

CEREALS AND GRAINS

Roots and Tubers

ROOTS AND TUBERS

Roots and Tubers are said to one of the most ordinary of foods but with the addition of flavourful herbs and spices, which is often the case in Indian cooking, these humble, earthy vegetables are transformed into the most delicious dishes.

Potatoes are one of the world's most important food crops. Easy to grow, inexpensive and subtantial, they become gastronomic delights in the hands of expert cooks.

In Indian cooking, potatoes are often cooked in their skins, which are enriched with vitamins. They are also often cubed and then prepared with spices. When a recipe calls for potato cubes, cut them accordingly and leave in a bowl of water so that they will not dry out.

Roots and tubers keep well in a cool, dry place but they should be used as soon as possible after they are cut so as not to lose their essential vitamins.

Roots and Tubers and their Nutrient Contents

Calories	★ ★ ★ ★
Protein	★
Fat	—
Calcium	★
Iron	★
Vitamin A	—
Vitamin B Complex	★
Vitamin C	—
Fibre	★ ★

None	—	Fair	★ ★ ★
Negligible	★	Good	★ ★ ★ ★
Some	★ ★	Very Good	★ ★ ★ ★ ★

ROOTS AND TUBERS

DRY POTATO TARKARI (Punjab)

Serves: 6   *Preparation: 10 minutes   Cooking Time: 20 minutes*
Kcal/serve: 323

Ingredients:

- 4 big potatoes, *unpeeled and cut into cubes*
- ½ cup oil
- 1 teaspoon mustard seeds
- 1 onion, *chopped*
- 2 teaspoons salt
- 2 teaspoons turmeric powder
- 2 teaspoons chilli powder
- 1 teaspoon sugar
- 1 teaspoon chopped fresh mint or coriander leaves
- 1 tablespoon green mango powder or lemon juice
- 3 medium-size tomatoes, *sliced*
- 1 teaspoon garam masala powder

Method:

Wash and drain potato cubes.

Heat oil and fry mustard seeds on medium heat. When seeds begin to pop, add potato cubes, onion, salt and turmeric powder. Fry till potato cubes turn light brown.

Add ½ cup water, chilli powder and sugar. Fry till mixture becomes dry, then add some water for gravy. Continue to cook with pan covered.

When potato cubes are tender, add mint (or coriander leaves), mango powder (or lemon juice) and cook till mixture turns dry. Add tomato slices.

Stir in garam masala powder and mix well before removing from heat.

POTATO WITH SPINACH (Maharastra)

Serves: 6 *Preparation: 10 minutes* *Cooking Time: 15 minutes*
Kcal/serve: 114

Ingredients:

1	lb (455 g) spinach
1	cup potato cubes
2	teaspoons salt
2	tablespoons oil
½	teaspoon black mustard seeds
½	teaspoon cummin seeds
2	medium-size onions, *chopped*
1	teaspoon turmeric powder
1	teaspoon coriander powder
2	teaspoons cummin seed powder
1	teaspoon sugar
4	fresh red chillies, *chopped*
4	teaspoons nutmeg powder

Method:

Wash spinach thoroughly. Chop roughly and add 1 teaspoon salt. Mix thoroughly.

Wash potato cubes and set aside.

Heat oil on medium heat and fry black mustard seeds and cummin seeds till they splutter.

Add the potato cubes, onion, the remaining teaspoon salt and turmeric powder. When potato cubes turn light brown, add ½ cup water.

Add coriander powder, cummin seed powder, sugar and chopped chillies. Fry till mixture smells fragrant.

Add spinach, mixing it well with the fried ingredients. Continue to cook with pan covered. Stir spinach occasionally till it is dry, then sprinkle with nutmeg powder before removing from the fire.

Serve with chapati or rice.

POTATO MATTAR RASA (Uttar Pradesh)

Serves: 6   Preparation: 20 minutes   Cooking Time: 30 minutes
              Kcal/serve: 192

Ingredients:

- 3   fresh red chillies
- 1   large onion
- 2   teaspoons pounded ginger
- 3   tablespoons oil or ghee
- 1   teaspoon turmeric powder
- 2   teaspoons coriander powder
- 2   teaspoons salt
- 2   teaspoons sugar
- 2   cups potato cubes, *skin removed*
- 2   large ripe tomatoes, *peeled and chopped*
- ½   cup yogurt, *beaten*
- 1   teaspoon garam masala powder
- 1   cup green peas
- 2   tablespoons chopped coriander leaves

Method:

Using a little water, grind chillies, onion and ginger to a smooth paste.

Heat oil (or ghee) on medium heat. Fry ground ingredients, turmeric powder, coriander powder, salt, sugar and ½ cup water for about 5 minutes. Add 2 cups hot water and cook for a further 15 minutes, covered. Add potato cubes.

When potato cubes are half-cooked, add chopped tomatoes. Cook for a few minutes.

Add the beaten yogurt, mixing it with a little water, if necessary, so that it forms a smooth paste.

Simmer till mixture becomes thick, then add garam masala powder, peas and chopped coriander leaves. Mix well.

Serve with rice or bread.

* *If peas are very young and tender, they can be put in together with the potatoes.*

Potato Dom

ROOTS AND TUBERS

POTATO DOM (Bengal)

Serves: 6   Preparation: 10 minutes   Cooking Time: ½ hour
Kcal/serve: 217

Ingredients:

- 1 lb (455 g) cauliflower
- 3 teaspoons turmeric powder
- 2 teaspoons salt
- ¼ cup oil for frying
- 2 or 3 bay leaves
- ½ teaspoon cummin seeds
- 2 teaspoons chilli powder
- 1 teaspoon pounded ginger or ginger powder
- 1 onion, *pounded*
- 1 teaspoon sugar
- ½ cup yogurt
- 2 teaspoons cummin seed powder, *roasted*
- 2 teaspoons ghee
- 2 tomatoes, *sliced*
- 2 tablespoons green peas
- 1 teaspoon garam masala

Method:

Wash and peel potatoes. Using a fork, prick peeled potatoes all over and marinate them in a mixture of 1 teaspoon turmeric powder and 2 teaspoons salt for 10 minutes.

Deep-fry marinated potatoes in oil till brown. Remove and set aside.

In the same pan, fry bay leaves and cummin seeds for 1 minute, then add remaining 2 teaspoons turmeric powder, chilli powder, pounded ginger (or ginger powder) pounded onion, sugar, yogurt and ½ teacup cold water.

Fry for 5 minutes till mixture smells fragrant. Add 4 cups water and the fried potatoes. Cover pan and leave to cook on medium heat.

When potatoes are cooked and gravy is thick, stir in roasted cummin seed powder, ghee, sliced tomatoes, green peas and garam masala.

Remove from heat and serve with plain white rice, chapati or loochi.

STEAMED POTATO DUM (Kashmir)

Serves: 6   Preparation: ½ hour   Cooking Time: 20 minutes
Kcal/serve: 177

Ingredients:

- 30 small-size new potatoes
- 6 small onions, *chopped roughly*
- 1 teaspoon chopped ginger
- 2 teaspoons chopped garlic
- 1 tablespoon lemon juice
- 3 tablespoons oil or ghee
- 2 sticks cinnamon, each approx 1 inch (2.5 cm) long
- 3 cardamoms, *pounded*
- 2 teaspoons turmeric powder
- 2 teaspoons salt
- 2 teaspoons sugar
- 5 fresh green chillies, *sliced and seeded*
- ½ teaspoon garam masala powder
- 2 tablespoons chopped coriander leaves
- ½ cup beaten yogurt
- 2 teaspoons cummin seed powder, *roasted*

Method:

Wash unpeeled potatoes and boil in a saucepan till three-quarters cooked. Drain off water and peel potatoes. Prick little holes all over each boiled potato.

Grind onion, ginger and garlic with lemon juice and 2 tablespoons water till it becomes a smooth puree.

In a pan, heat oil (or ghee) on medium heat. Fry cinnamon sticks and cardamoms for a few minutes. Add ground ingredients, turmeric powder, 1 teaspoon salt, 1 teaspoon sugar, chillies and ½ cup water. Fry till mixture smells fragrant.

Put in potatoes and continue frying for a few minutes. Add 3 cups water and continue to cook with pan covered.

When potatoes are soft, add garam masala and chopped coriander leaves. Mix well before removing from fire. (There should be some thick gravy left in the pan.)

To the beaten yogurt, add roasted cummin seed powder, the remaining teaspoon salt and 1 teaspoon sugar. Mix well.

Serve Steamed Potato Dum and the yogurt mixture, separately, with chapati or bread.

ROOTS AND TUBERS

POTATO KIMA CURRY (Parsee)

Serves: 6   Preparation: 10 minutes   Cooking Time: 10 minutes
Kcal/serve: 269

Ingredients:

- ½ cup ghee or oil
- 4 medium-size potatoes, *cut into cubes*
- 2 teaspoons chopped ginger
- 1 onion, *chopped*
- 2 teaspoons salt
- 1 teaspoon sugar
- 5 fresh green chillies, *ground*
- 1 tablespoon beaten yogurt
- 1 cup green peas, *coarsely ground*
- 2 teaspoons roasted cummin seed powder
- 1 teaspoon garam masala
- 2 tomatoes, *sliced*

Method:

Heat ghee (or oil) on medium heat. When hot, fry potatoes till light brown. Add onion, ginger, salt, sugar, ground chillies, yogurt and ½ cup water. Cook till mixture is dry.

Add ground peas, roasted cummin seed powder, sliced tomatoes and garam masala. Cook till potato cubes are tender.

Serve with chapati or rice.

Note: You can substitute onion with asafoetida powder.

ROOTS AND TUBERS

Yam Dalna

ROOTS AND TUBERS

YAM DALNA (Bengal)

Serves: 6   Preparation: 10 minutes   Cooking Time: 10 minutes
Kcal/serve: 277

Ingredients:

- ½ lb (255 g) yam, *unpeeled and cut into cubes*
- 3 teaspoons turmeric powder
- 3 teaspoons salt
- 2 medium-size potatoes, *peeled and cut into cubes*
- ½ cup oil
- 1 teaspoon small cummin seeds
- 1 onion, *chopped*
- 2 teaspoons chilli powder
- 1 teaspoon sugar
- 1 teaspoon cummin seed powder
- 2 tablespoons beaten yogurt
- 1 teaspoon garam masala powder

Method:

Wash and drain yam cubes, then rub in a little turmeric powder and salt.

Heat oil and fry potato cubes on medium heat till light brown. Remove and set aside.

Now fry yam cubes till light brown. Remove and set aside.

In the same pan, fry cummin seeds till they pop. Put in chopped onion and fry till light brown. Add ½ cup water, chilli powder, sugar, 2 teaspoons turmeric powder, cummin seed powder and yogurt. Fry till mixture turns dry.

Add yam and potato cubes and 2 cups water. Continue to cook, with pan covered, till potato is tender. Add garam masala before removing from fire. (Gravy should be quite thick.)

Yellow Vegetables, Gourds and Squashes

YELLOW VEGETABLES, GOURDS AND SQUASHES

This class of vegetables is rich in calcium, iron, Vitamin A, Vitamin B Complex, Vitamin C and fibre. They are also rich in natural sugars and fructose sugars, both of which supply the body with energy.

With lots of Vitamin A, body cells grow well and you show a high resistance to infections. Vitamin B is good for digestion, keeps nerves stable and helps a flagging appetite.

One of the most popular yellow vegetables is the carrot. Rich in carotene, it is said to be good for the eyesight. Gourds and squashes are fleshy and have a high water content. They supply fibre and roughage, necessary for the natural elimination of body wastes and to regulate the system.

Yellow Vegetables and their Nutrient Contents

Calories	★
Protein	★
Fat	—
Calcium	★
Iron	★
Vitamin A	★
Vitamin B Complex	—
Vitamin C	★ ★
Fibre	★ ★ ★

None	—	Fair	★ ★ ★
Negligible	★	Good	★ ★ ★ ★
Some	★ ★	Very Good	★ ★ ★ ★ ★

YELLOW VEGETABLES, GOURDS AND SQUASHES

DRUM STICK CURRY (Madras)

Serves: 6   *Preparation: 20 minutes*   *Cooking Time: ½ hour*
Kcal/serve: 323

Ingredients:

- 20 drumsticks
- ½ coconut, *grated*
- 3 teaspoons salt
- 3 teaspoons chilli powder
- 2 teaspoons turmeric powder
- 1 teaspoon sugar
- 2 teaspoons coriander powder
- 1 tablespoon mashed panir
- 2 tablespoons oil
- 1 teaspoon fenugreek
- 1 large onion, *chopped*
- 1 teaspoon cummin seed powder, *roasted*
- 3 teaspoons lemon juice

Method:

Remove skin of drumsticks by scraping with a knife. Cut drumsticks into 2 inch (5 inch) lengths and set aside.

Mix grated coconut with 1 cup water; squeeze to obtain a thick milk. Strain and set aside. Add 1 cup water to coconut and squeeze to obtain a thin milk. Strain and and set aside.

Boil drumstick pieces in the thin coconut milk with salt, chilli powder, turmeric powder, sugar and coriander powder.

When drumstick is half-cooked, add the thick coconut milk and the mashed panir. Cook till drumstick is tender.

Heat oil in pan and fry fenugreek till slightly brown. Add onion and fry till light brown.

Put in the cooked drumstick pieces, roasted cummin seed powder and lemon juice. Mix well.

When gravy is quite thick, remove from fire.

YELLOW VEGETABLES, GOURDS AND SQUASHES

BITTER GOURD VAJI (Punjab)

Serves: 6   *Preparation: 10 minutes*   *Cooking Time: 20 minutes*   *Seasoning: 30 minutes*
Kcal/serve: 212

Ingredients:

- 2 medium-size bitter gourds
- 2 teaspoons salt
- 1 teaspoon turmeric powder
- ½ cup cooking oil
- 4 dried red chillies
- 1 teaspoon black cummin seeds (nygella)
- 1 onion, *chopped*
- 1 teaspoon chilli powder

Method:

Slice bitter gourd into thin rounds; wash and season with salt and turmeric powder. Let stand for 30 minutes.

After bitter gourd slices have been seasoned, squeeze to extract and discard juice. Dry the slices with paper towels.

Heat oil. Fry dried red chillies, black cummin seeds and chopped onion on medium heat for a few minutes.

Add bitter gourd slices and chilli powder. When slices turn brown and crispy, remove from fire.

YELLOW VEGETABLES, GOURDS AND SQUASHES

LONG WATERY PUMPKIN KOPTA (Gujerat)

Serves: 6   *Preparation: 10 minutes   Cooking Time: 30 minutes*
Kcal/serve: 179

Ingredients:

1   medium-size pumpkin
4   teaspoons salt
1   cup beshan (horse gram dhall) powder
3   teaspoons chilli powder
1   tablespoon plain flour
1   cup cooking oil
2   teaspoons cummin seed powder
2   sticks cinnamon, each about about 1 inch (2.5 cm long)
3 or 4 cardamoms
2   teaspoons sugar
2   tomatoes, *sliced*
1   onion, *ground*
2   teaspoons pounded ginger
2   teaspoons turmeric powder
1   teaspoon corn flour
1   teaspoon garam masala

Method:

Peel pumpkin; wash and cut into fine slices. Rub with 1 teaspoon salt, then squeeze and discard juice.

Mix beshan powder with 1 teaspoon chilli powder and plain flour. Add pumpkin and a little water for a thick paste. Form round, flat patties.

Heat oil. Fry patties, a few at a time, on medium heat till golden-brown. Remove and drain; set aside.

In the same pan, put in cummin seeds, cinnamon and cardamoms. Fry for a few minutes and then add 1 teacup water.

Put in chilli powder, cummin seed powder, the remaining 3 teaspoons salt, sugar, tomato slices, onion, ginger and turmeric powder.

When mixture turns dry, add the patties (kopta) and 2 cups water. Cook for 10 minutes.

Mix corn flour with 3 teaspoons water; add to pan for thickening.

Stir in garam masala just before removing from fire.

YELLOW VEGETABLES, GOURDS AND SQUASHES

SWEET PUMPKIN CHOKKA (Bengal)

Serves: 8   *Preparation: 20 minutes   Cooking Time: 30 minutes*
Kcal/serve: 356   Soaking of chana: Overnight

Ingredients:

- 2 tablespoons horse gram (chana), *left whole and unpeeled*
- 1 cup cooking oil
- 2 lbs (910 g) sweet pumpkin, *cut into medium-size cubes*
- 2 large potatoes, *cut into cubes*
- 1 teaspoon cummin seeds
- 3 sticks cinnamon, each 1 in (2.5 cm) long
- 4 cardamoms
- 2 teaspoons chopped ginger
- 2 medium-size onions, *chopped*
- 1 tablespoon chilli powder
- 2 teaspoons cummin seed powder
- 2 teaspoons turmeric powder
- 2 teaspoons sugar
- 3 teaspoons salt
- 1 teaspoon garam masala powder

Method:

Soak the horse gram (chana) in water overnight. After it has been soaked, wash and boil till half-cooked.

Heat oil on medium heat and fry potato cubes till golden brown. Remove and set aside.

In the same pan, fry pumpkin cubes, a few at a time, till they turn light brown. Remove and set aside.

Fry cummin seeds, cinnamon, cardamoms, ginger and onions till slightly brown. Pour in ½ cup water; add chilli powder, cummin seed powder, turmeric powder, sugar, salt and horse gram. Fry till all water is absorbed with spices.

Add 3 cups water and put in the fried potato cubes. Cover pan and continue to simmer till vegetables are tender.

When gravy is quite thick, mix in garam masala powder with the cooked vegetables just before removing from fire.

Sweet Pumpkin Chokka

YELLOW VEGETABLES, GOURDS AND SQUASHES

CARROT TARKARI (Gujerat)

Makes: 12   Preparation: 10 minutes   Cooking Time: 20 minutes
Kcal/serve: 234   Soaking of dhall: Overnight

Ingredients:

- 1 tablespoon horse gram (chana)
- 2 cups grated carrot
- ½ cup cooking oil
- 3 dried red chillies
- 1 teaspoon mustard seeds
- 2 teaspoons salt
- 1 teaspoon sugar
- 2 teaspoons chilli powder
- 2 tablespoons ground coconut
- 1 onion, *chopped*

Method:

Soak the horse gram overnight; wash and boil till half-cooked.

Wash and drain grated carrot.

Heat oil and fry dried red chillies and mustard seeds till brown. Add grated carrot, salt, sugar, chilli powder, ground coconut, chopped onion and horse gram. Fry for a few minutes and then cover pan, keeping heat low.

When mixture turns dry, add 2 cups water. Cover pan and leave to simmer on low heat till carrot and horse gram are completely cooked.

Turn heat to medium and fry mixture for a few minutes before removing from fire.

YELLOW VEGETABLES, GOURDS AND SQUASHES

WHITE RADISH TARKARI (Bihar)

Serves: 6   Preparation: ½ hour   Cooking Time: ½ hour
Kcal/serve: 284

Ingredients:

- 2 tablespoons horse gram (chana), *left whole and unpeeled*
- 2 large radishes, *grated*
- 2 teaspoons salt
- ½ cup oil
- 2 large potatoes, *cut into cubes*
- 1 teaspoon black cummin seeds
- 3 dried red chillies
- 2 teaspoons sugar
- 2 teaspoons chilli powder
- 1 tablespoon ground coconut
- 2 teaspoons corn flour

Method:

Soak the horse gram (chana) overnight. After it has been soaked, wash and boil till half-cooked.

Rub salt into the grated radish, mixing thoroughly. Squeeze radish and discard juice.

Heat oil and fry potato cubes on medium heat till brown. Remove and set aside.

Fry black cummin seeds and dred red chillies in the same pan till brown.

Add radish, sugar, chilli powder and coconut. Fry for a few minutes, then add fried potato cubes and horse gram. Continue to cook with pan covered, stirring frequently.

When radish and potato cubes are tender, add corn flour mixed with ¼ cup water. Fry mixture for a few minutes and remove from fire when it turns dry.

Green Vegetables and Vegetable Fruit

GREEN VEGETABLES AND VEGETABLE FRUIT

Leafy green vegetables and vegetable fruit are laden with vitamins and minerals and are especially rich in calcium, iron, potassium and vitamins A, B, C, E, and K. Greens also provide roughage, necessary in the elimination of body wastes.

Calcium helps build bones, teeth and nails. It is said to be good for the nerves, too. Iron helps the blood carry oxygen to all our body cells; an iron-deficient diet can result in anaemia and listlessness. Potassium is a muscle mineral – important to such functions as heart action. The best vegetables for roughage are the cabbage, cauliflower, tomato and eggplant.

Spinach is rich in Vitamin E and the chilli, which is used so often in Indian cooking, is rich in Vitamin C.

Green vegetables should be eaten at their freshest, preferably the day they are bought. In fact, from the moment they are picked, vegetables like peas and beans start converting their sugars into starch.

Green Vegetables and their Nutrient Contents

Calories	★
Protein	★
Fat	—
Calcium	★ ★
Iron	★ ★
Vitamin A	★ ★ ★
Vitamin B Complex	★
Vitamin C	★ ★
Fibre	★ ★ ★

None	—	Fair	★ ★ ★
Negligible	★	Good	★ ★ ★ ★
Some	★ ★	Very Good	★ ★ ★ ★ ★

GREEN VEGETABLES AND VEGETABLE FRUIT

BATI CHORANO (Bengal)

Serves: 6 *Preparation: 10 minutes* *Cooking Time: ½ hour*
Kcal/serve: 238

Ingredients:

- ½ teacup small cauliflower cubes, from 2 florets
- ½ teacup French beans, cut into 1 in (2.5 cm) lengths
- ½ teacup carrot cubes
- ½ teacup small potato cubes, from 2 potatoes
- ½ teacup oil
- A few sprigs spring onions, *chopped*
- 2 teaspoons salt
- 1 teaspoon sugar
- 2 teaspoons chilli powder
- 1 teaspoon turmeric powder
- 4 fresh green chillies
- A few chopped coriander leaves
- 2 teaspoons dry mustard seed powder

Method:

Wash all vegetables and drain off water.

Heat oil and fry spring onions till light brown.

Mix cauliflower, French beans, carrot and potato with salt, sugar, chilli powder, turmeric powder, fresh chillies, coriander leaves and fried spring onion with the heated oil in the pan. Add 1 teacup water.

Simmer till vegetables are cooked and dry. Add mustard seed powder and continue to simmer for a few minutes before removing from fire.

Serve with plain rice.

Note: If you're using a pressure cooker, vegetables can be cooked within 5 minutes.

GREEN VEGETABLES AND VEGETABLE FRUIT

CAULIFLOWER WITH COCONUT (Kerala)

Serves: 6   *Preparation: 20 minutes*   *Cooking Time: 20 minutes*
Kcal/serve: 264

Ingredients:

1	lb (455 g) cauliflower
½	cup cooking oil or melted ghee
4	dried red chillies
1	teaspoon mustard seeds
2	teaspoons salt
1	teaspoon sugar
2	teaspoons pounded ginger
1	large onion, *chopped*
4	fresh green chillies, *chopped*
½	cup ground coconut
½	cup green peas

Method:

Cut cauliflower into thin slices; wash and set aside.

Heat oil (or ghee) in a deep pan. Fry dried chillies and mustard seeds till they start to splutter.

Add sliced cauliflower, salt, sugar, ginger, onion, chillies and ½ cup water. Cover pan and continue to cook till almost all liquid is absorbed.

Add coconut and 1 cup water; simmer till cauliflower is cooked. Add lemon juice.

Put in green peas and simmer for a few minutes before removing from fire.

Serve with bread or chapati.

GREEN VEGETABLES AND VEGETABLE FRUIT

CAULIFLOWER AND MUSHROOM (Sindhi)

Serves: 8   Preparation: 10 minutes   Cooking Time: 30 minutes
Kcal/serve: 384

Ingredients:

1	lb (455 g) cauliflower	
1	lb (455 g) carrots	
2	potatoes	*cut into cubes*
1	large capsicum	
¼	lb (115 g) mushrooms	

4   fresh green chillies, *cut into halves*
1   cup cooking oil or melted ghee
10 small shallots, *left whole*
4   dried red chillies
2   teaspoons chopped ginger
½   cup green peas
    A few coriander leaves, *chopped*
2   teaspoons salt
1   teaspoon sugar
3   tomatoes, *sliced*
2   teaspoons corn flour or plain flour

Method:

Cut cauliflower, carrots, potatoes, capsicum and mushrooms into cubes. Wash vegetables and mushroooms separately; drain and set aside.

Heat oil (or ghee) in a deep pan and fry potatoes and carrots on medium heat till light brown. Remove from fire and set aside.

In the same pan, fry ginger and dried chillies till they turn light brown. Add mushrooms and continue frying for a few minutes.

Put in the fried carrot and potato cubes. Add shallots, cauliflower, salt, sugar, sliced tomatoes and chopped green chillies. Continue to cook with pan covered, stirring frequently.

When vegetables are dry, add 1 cup water. Continue to cook with pan covered.

When vegetables are completely cooked, add green peas and coriander leaves.

Mix corn flour (or plain flour) with 4 teaspoons water. Add flour mixture to pan and stir in with the cooked vegetables, mixing thoroughly.

When mixture is quite dry, remove from heat.

GREEN VEGETABLES AND VEGETABLE FRUIT

CAULIFLOWER KORMA WITH GARNISH (Bengal)

Serves: 8　　Preparation: 20 minutes　Cooking Time: 20 minutes
　　　　　　Kcal/serve: 313

Ingredients:

for Cauliflower Korma:
1　large head of cauliflower
½　cup cooking oil
3　teaspoons salt
4　sticks cinnamon, each 1 inch (2.5 cm) long
5 or 6 cardamoms
1　cup almonds, *peeled and pounded or ground to a paste**
1　tablespoon raisins, *pounded*
5　fresh green chillies, *pounded or ground*
2　teaspoons sugar
1　cup beaten yogurt

Method:

Cut cauliflower into 8 pieces. Wash and set aside.

Heat oil (or ghee) and fry cauliflower on medium heat with 1 teaspoon salt.

When cauliflower pieces turn light brown, remove from pan and set aside.

Fry cinnamon and cardamoms in the same pan. Add 1 cup water with the ground almonds, raisins and pounded chilli. Cook till all water is absorbed.

Add the fried cauliflower pieces and continue to cook with pan covered, stirring frequently.

Add the remaining salt, the sugar, yogurt and 1 cup water.

When cauliflower is tender and gravy is thick, remove from fire. (Do not overcook.)

* Soak almonds in hot water for three hours before removing skin.

GREEN VEGETABLES AND VEGETABLE FRUIT

Ingredients:

for Garnish:
- 4 potatoes
- Salt and black pepper to taste
- 4 tomatoes
- 1 teacup green peas
- 5 fresh red chillies, *left whole*

Method:

Boil potatoes in their skins till three-quarters cooked; peel when cooled. Rub in salt and black pepper and fry or bake potatoes till golden brown.

Slice off and discard tomato ends. Rub tomatoes with a little salt and black pepper; bake for about 5 minutes.

Serve Cauliflower Korma in a deep dish. Garnish with the cooked potatoes, tomatoes, peas and red chillies.

Note: You may choose to serve Cauliflower Dom without Garnish.

GREEN VEGETABLES AND VEGETABLE FRUIT

Cauliflower Korma (top), Mixed Vegetables (middle) and Panir Devil Curry (below)

GREEN VEGETABLES AND VEGETABLE FRUIT

PANIR DEVIL CURRY (Bengal)

Makes: 10   *Preparation: 1 hour*   *Cooking Time: ½ hour*
Kcal/serve: 348

Ingredients:

- 1 lb (455 g) cauliflower
- 2 teaspoons salt
- 2 teaspoons turmeric powder
- 2 teacups panir
- 4 teaspoons flour
- ½ teacup melted ghee
- 1 drop of orange food colouring
- 1 teaspoon cummin seeds
- 4 pieces cinnamon, each about 1 in or 2.5 cm long
- 6 cardamoms
- 3 teaspoons chilli powder
- 2 teaspoons cummin seed powder
- 1 teaspoon sugar
- ¼ cup beaten yogurt
- 1 teaspoon garam masala
- ½ cup green peas
- 2 tomatoes, *sliced*

Method:

Cut cauliflower into big pieces; wash and drain off water. Rub cauliflower with 1 teaspoon salt and a little turmeric powder.

Mix three-quarters of the panir with ½ teaspoon salt, flour and 4 teaspoons ghee. Knead well and set aside.

Mix the remaining salt with the rest of the panir. Add a drop of orange food colouring. Mix well and then shape into 10 balls of equal size.

Divide plain panir into 10 portions. Shape each portion like a half-boiled egg with a hollow. Fill orange-coloured panir in the hollow so that it resembles a half egg.

Heat oil (or ghee) on medium heat. Fry cauliflower pieces till golden brown. Remove. Fry panir 'eggs' till light brown. Remove.
In the same pan, fry cummin seeds, cinnamon and cardamoms. Add 1 cup water, chilli powder, cummin seed powder, turmeric powder, salt, sugar, yogurt and cauliflower.

When mixture turns a little dry, add 2 cups water for gravy. Add the fried panir 'eggs' and cook for a few minutes. Add garam masala, green peas and tomatoes; mix well and remove from fire.

GREEN VEGETABLES AND VEGETABLE FRUIT

CABBAGE DOM (Punjab)

Serves: 6   Preparation: 10 minutes   Cooking Time: 20 minutes
Kcal/serve: 313

Ingredients:

- 1 large cabbage
- 4 large potatoes, *cut into cubes*
- ½ cup ghee or oil
- 3 bay leaves
- 1 teaspoon sweet cummin seeds
- 4 sticks cinnamon, each approx. 1 inch (2.5 cm) long
- 4 cardamoms, *pounded*
- 2 teaspoons salt
- 1 teaspoon sugar
- 2 teaspoons turmeric powder
- 2 teaspoons chilli powder
- 2 teaspoons sweet cummin seed powder
- 2 teaspoons pounded ginger
- ¼ cup beaten yogurt
- ½ cup green peas
- 1 teaspoon garam masala

Method:

Wash and cut cabbage leaves into bite-size pieces. Wash potato cubes.

Heat oil and fry potato cubes on medium heat till light brown. Remove and set aside.

In the same pan, fry bay leaves, sweet cummin seeds, cinnamon and cardamoms till seeds pop.

Add cabbage, salt, sugar, turmeric powder, chilli powder, cummin seed powder, pounded ginger and ½ cup water. Cook for a few minutes with pan covered.

Add fried potato cubes and yogurt. Fry mixture till liquid is completely absorbed, then add 2 cups water. Continue to cook, with pan covered, till potatoes are tender. Add green peas.

Mix the corn flour with a little water and add it to the mixture.

Add garam masala before removing from fire. (Gravy should be quite thick.)

GREEN VEGETABLES AND VEGETABLE FRUIT

CABBAGE DALNA (Bengal)

Serves: 6   Preparation: 20 minutes   Cooking Time: 30 minutes
Kcal/serve: 302

Ingredients:

- 1 large cabbage
- 2 potatoes, *cut into cubes*
- ½ cup oil or ghee
- 2 teaspoons salt
- 1 teaspoon black cummin seeds or mustard seeds
- 1 teaspoon sugar
- 6 fresh red chillies
- ½ cup unsweetened milk
- ½ cup green peas
- 2 teaspoons corn flour
- 2 tomatoes, *halved and then sliced*

Method:

Cut cabbage leaves into bite-size pieces; wash, drain and set aside.

Wash potato cubes with a little salt; fry in oil (or ghee) till light brown. Remove from fire and set aside.

In the same pan, fry cabbage with black cummin seeds, salt, sugar and red chillies. Add the potato cubes and continue to fry mixture till cabbage is half-cooked.

Add milk and 2 cups water. Continue to cook mixture on medium heat with pan covered.

When potato and cabbage are completely cooked, add green peas. Stir in the corn flour, mixed with a little water. Add tomato slices before removing from fire.

GREEN VEGETABLES AND VEGETABLE FRUIT

EGGPLANT PUREE (Punjab)

Serves: 6   Preparation: 20 minutes   Cooking Time: 10 minutes
Kcal/serve: 115

Ingredients:

- 4 large eggplants
- 2 tablespoons oil
- 3 medium-size onions, *chopped*
- 2 teaspoons chilli powder
- 1 teaspoon coriander powder
- 1 teaspoon cummin seed powder
- 2 teaspoons salt
- 1 teaspoon sugar, *optional*
- 4 large ripe tomatoes, *chopped*
- 4 spring onions, *chopped finely*
- 2 tablespoons finely chopped coriander leaves

Method:

Bake eggplants over gas flame, on hot coals or under grill till skins are blackened and flesh is soft to the touch.

When eggplants are cool enough to handle, peel the skins off while holding them under running water.

Mash or roughly chop the peeled eggplants.

Heat oil and fry chopped onions on medium heat till lightly brown. Add chilli powder, coriander powder, cummin seed powder and ½ cup water.

Add salt, and sugar (if you wish). Fry mixture for a few minutes and then add mashed eggplant and chopped tomatoes.

Cook on medium heat till all liquid evaporates and mixture becomes a thick puree.

Add the spring onions and coriander leaves. Mix well before removing from fire.

Serve Eggplant Puree with chapati, paratha or plain rice.

EGGPLANT BARATHA (Maharastra)

Serves: 6   *Preparation: 15 minutes*   *Cooking Time: 10 minutes*
            Kcal/serve: 108

Ingredients:

- 4   large eggplants
- 2   tablespoons oil
- 2   teaspoons shredded ginger
- 2   onions, *chopped*
- 2   teaspoons chilli powder
- ½   cup grated coconut
- 1   teaspoon sugar
- 3   teaspoons salt
- 3   tomato slices
- 1   tablespoon mustard powder

Method:

Bake eggplants under a grill till skins are blackened and flesh is soft to the touch. Peel and discard skins.

Mash peeled eggplants. Set aside.

Heat oil. Fry ginger and onions till light brown. Add mashed eggplant, chilli powder, grated coconut, sugar, salt, tomatoes and mustard powder. Fry till mixture turns dry.

GREEN VEGETABLES AND VEGETABLE FRUIT

FRENCH BEANS AND MUSHROOM BHAJI   (Punjab)

Serves: 6   *Preparation: 20 minutes   Cooking Time: 20 minutes*
             Kcal/serve: 240

Ingredients:

1   lb (455 g) French beans
½   lb (275 g) mushrooms
½   cup cooking oil
1   large onion, *chopped*
2   teaspoons chopped ginger
2   teaspoons salt
1   teaspoon sugar
4   fresh red chillies, *chopped*
2   teaspoons chilli powder
2   tomatoes, *sliced*
2   teaspoons soya sauce

Method:

Wash and slice French beans into 1 inch (2.5 cm) lengths.

Cut mushrooms into fine slices; wash and set aside.

Fry onion and ginger till light brown. Add mushrooms, salt, sugar, red chillies and a little water.

Fry for a few minutes; add beans and chilli powder. Stir well and cover pan, lowering heat to low.

When beans are soft, add tomato slices and soya sauce. Cook for a few minutes before removing from heat.

GREEN VEGETABLES AND VEGETABLE FRUIT

FRENCH BEANS WITH COCONUT (Gujerat)

Serves: 4   Preparation: 10 minutes   Cooking Time: 20 minutes
Kcal/serve: 225

Ingredients:

- 1 lb (455 g) French beans
- ¼ cup cooking oil
- 1 large onion, *chopped*
- 2 teaspoons salt
- ½ teaspoon sugar
- 4 fresh red chillies, *chopped*
- ¼ cup ground coconut
- 2 tomatoes, *sliced*

Method:

Cut French beans into 2 inch (5 cm) lengths; wash and drain.

Heat oil and fry onion on medium heat till soft.

Add French beans, salt, sugar and chopped chillies. Fry till beans are half-cooked.

Add the ground coconut, ½ cup water and sugar. Cover pan and continue to simmer on low heat. Stir mixture occasionally.

Remove from heat when beans are fully-cooked and mixture is dry.

GREEN VEGETABLES AND VEGETABLE FRUIT

Eggplant Dolma

GREEN VEGETABLES AND VEGETABLE FRUIT

EGGPLANT DOLMA (Bengal)

Serves: 6   **Preparation:** ½ hour   **Cooking Time:** ½ hour
             Kcal/serve: 288

Ingredients:

- 6 large eggplants
- 1 tablespoon plain flour
- 1 cup oil
- 2 medium-size potatoes ⎫
- 1 carrot   ⎬ *cut into cubes*
- 2 florets cauliflower ⎭
- 3 teaspoons salt
- 1 teaspoon sugar
- 3 teaspoons chilli powder
- 2 teaspoons pounded ginger
- 2 teaspoons fried cummin seed powder
- 3 or 4 bunches coriander leaves, *chopped*
- A few toothpicks

Method:

Wash eggplants, remove stalks and slice off about ½ in (1 cm) from ends. Wash again and set aside.

Hollow out eggplants by scraping out pulp. Set pulp aside.
Soak hollowed-out eggplants and sliced ends in water.

Mix flour with a little water to form a smooth batter. Set aside.

Heat ¼ cup oil and fry potato, carrot and cauliflower cubes with salt, sugar, chilli powder, pounded ginger and fried cummin seed powder on medium heat till half-cooked.

Add eggplant pulp and simmer mixture over low heat, with pan covered.

When vegetables are completely cooked, add coriander leaves. Continue to cook till mixture turns dry.

Remove eggplants and sliced ends from water. Dry them thoroughly with a paper towel.

Fill each hollowed-out eggplant with the fried vegetable mixture.

Dip each sliced end in the batter. Cover eggplants with battered sliced ends, using toothpicks to secure.

Heat the rest of the oil on medium heat and fry stuffed eggplants, a few at a time, till they turn brown.

Remove eggplants from pan and drain off excess oil.

GREEN VEGETABLES AND VEGETABLE FRUIT

FRIED BEANS (Karnataka)

Serves: 6   Preparation: 20 minutes   Cooking Time: 20 minutes
Kcal/serve: 225

Ingredients:

- 8 snake beans or bottle beans
- 2 tablespoons cooking oil
- ½ teaspoon black mustard seeds
- 1 teaspoon finely grated ginger
- 1 large onion, *finely chopped*
- 1 teaspoon chilli powder
- 2 teaspoons salt
- 1 teaspoon turmeric powder
- 5 fresh red chillies, *chopped*
- 1 cup coconut milk
- 1 teaspoon garam masala powder
- 2 teaspoons lemon juice

Method:

Cut beans into 2 inch (5 cm) lengths, discarding ends. Wash and set aside.

Heat oil and fry mustard seeds on medium heat till they pop. Add ginger and onion and fry till light brown and soft. Add chilli powder.

Add sliced beans, salt, turmeric powder and chopped chillies. Fry for a few minutes and then add coconut milk. Add garam masala powder.

Continue to cook mixture, stirring occasionally till beans are tender and gravy is quite thick.

Stir in lemon juice just before removing from fire.

Serve Fried Beans with thosai or rice.

CABBAGE TARKARI (Bengal)

Serves: 4   *Preparation: 10 minutes   Cooking Time: 30 minutes*
            Kcal/serve: 397

Ingredients:

1½ lbs (680g) cabbage, *finely shredded*
2   large potatoes, *cut into cubes*
½   cup oil
1   teaspoon cummin seeds
2   teaspoons chilli powder
2   teaspoons cummin seed powder
1   teaspoon turmeric powder
1   teaspoon sugar
1   teaspoon pounded ginger
2   teaspoons salt
½   teaspoon garam masala
2   teaspoons plain flour
½   cup green peas

Method:

Wash and drain shredded cabbage and potato cubes.

Heat oil and fry potato cubes on medium heat till light brown. Remove and set aside.

In the same pan, fry cummin seeds till they pop. Add cabbage, chilli powder, cummin seed powder, turmeric powder, sugar, ginger and salt, stirring frequently till cabbage is half-cooked.

Add fried potato cubes. Stir well and cover pan, keeping heat low.

When potato and cabbage are cooked, add garam masala, plain flour and green peas. Cook till dry.

GREEN VEGETABLES AND VEGETABLE FRUIT

MIXED VEGETABLES (Sindhi)

Serves: 6   Preparation: 20 minutes   Cooking Time: ½ hour
Kcal/serve: 214

Ingredients:

- 2   large potatoes
- 2   large carrots
- 2   florets cauliflower
- 2   medium-size onions
- 1   tablespoon coriander powder
- 1   teaspoon turmeric powder
- 4   tablespoons oil or ghee
- 1   teaspoon finely grated ginger
- ½   cup chopped coriander leaves
- 2   ripe tomatoes, *sliced*
- 1   teaspoon sugar
- 1   cup yogurt
- 2   teaspoons salt
- 1   tablespoon lemon juice

Method:

Peel potatoes and carrots; cut into small cubes. Wash and set aside.

Cut cauliflower into cubes, wash and set aside.

Chop onions finely and mix with cauliflower, potato and carrot cubes. Sprinkle coriander powder and turmeric powder on the vegetables, tossing to mix well.

Leave to stand for 1 hour.

Heat oil (or ghee) in a pan; fry ginger till golden-brown. Add the mixed vegetables and fry for a few minutes.

Add half the amount of coriander leaves, tomato slices, sugar, yogurt, salt and chillies. Continue to cook covered till all vegetables are tender.

Remove from fire and garnish with the remaining amount of coriander leaves.

Serve hot with plain rice, pooris or chapati.

MIXED VEGETABLES WITH COCONUT (Kerala)

Serves: 6   Preparation: 20 minutes   Cooking Time: ½ hour
Kcal/serve: 255

Ingredients:

6 cups mixed vegetables, cut into julienne strips – carrots, French beans, pumpkin, potatoes, capsicum, eggplant, cauliflower, zucchini, unripe mangoes, etc.
- ½ cup freshly ground coconut or 3 tablespoons desiccated coconut
- 4 green chillies, *sliced*
- 2 teaspoons chopped garlic
- 1 medium-size onion
- 1 tablespoon oil
- 1 teaspoon mustard seeds
- 8 curry leaves
- ½ cup fresh green peas
- ½ cup thick coconut milk
- 2 teaspoons salt
- 1 tablespoon lemon juice

Method:

Boil each type of vegetable separately in a saucepan with just enough salted water to cover the strips. Add more water whenever necessary. Reserve liquid.

When vegetables are soft and tender (but not mushy), remove with a slotted spoon and set aside in a bowl.

Mix the ground coconut, chillies, cummin seeds, garlic and onion with a little water to form a smooth paste.

Heat oil in another pan and fry mustard seeds till they start to pop. Add curry leaves, all the boiled vegetables, peas, coconut milk and salt.

When mixture boils, leave it for a few minutes before removing from fire. Add lemon juice.
Serve with rice and thosai.

GREEN VEGETABLES AND VEGETABLE FRUIT

Unripe Fruit

UNRIPE FRUIT

Fruit is rich in Vitamin C and the Indian diet features it often, either as an accompaniment to the main meal in the form of raitas, pickles and chutneys, or cooked in a dish.

Chutneys, pickles and raitas are an important accompaniment to the main meal. Unlike salads, they are eaten in a small quantity to add just a slight touch of piquancy to curries and dhalls.

The most popular chutneys in India are made from mango, tomato, tamarind, fruits like apples, and leaves from the mint and coriander.

Pickles differ from chutneys in that they do not spoil and can be kept, if well-stored, even up to a couple of years. Raitas are yogurt-based and are a wonderful accompaniment to hot curry dishes.

In this section, unripe fruit is used in the cooking of delicious dishes.

Fruit and their Nutrient Contents

Calories	★ ★
Protein	—
Fat	—
Calcium	—
Iron	★
Vitamin A	★ ★ ★
Vitamin B Complex	—
Vitamin C	★ ★ ★ ★ ★
Fibre	★ ★ ★

None	—	Fair	★ ★ ★
Negligible	★	Good	★ ★ ★ ★
Some	★ ★	Very Good	★ ★ ★ ★ ★

UNRIPE FRUIT

GREEN BANANA KOPTA (Maharastra)

Makes: 20   *Preparation: 20 minutes   Cooking Time: ¾ hour*
             Kcal/serve: 189

Ingredients:

- 5 green unripe bananas
- 2 teaspoons salt
- 2 teaspoons sugar
- 2 teaspoons chilli powder or 4 fresh green chillies, *chopped*
- 2 teaspoons pounded ginger
- 1 teaspoon fried cummin seed powder
- A few coriander leaves, *chopped*
- 1 tablespoon plain flour
- 1 tablespoon horse gram dhall powder
- 1 medium-size onion, *chopped finely*
- 1 teaspoon garam masala powder
- 1 cup cooking oil

Method:

Peel bananas and boil in water till cooked; mash with salt, sugar, chilli powder (or chopped fresh green chillies), pounded ginger, fried cummin seed powder, coriander leaves, flour, horse gram dhall powder and chopped onion. Knead mixture thoroughly. Add garam masala powder.

Divide mixture into 20 equal portions. Shape each portion into a round, flat ping-pong ball.

Heat oil and fry balls on medium heat till golden brown. Remove and drain off excess oil.

Serve Banana Kopta with any sauce or chutney.

Note: If you prefer to cook Banana Kopta in a curry, follow the recipe for Horse Gram Dhall Kopta Curry.

UNRIPE FRUIT

Unripe Jackfruit Curry

UNRIPE FRUIT

UNRIPE JACKFRUIT CURRY (Bengal)

Serves: 10 Preparation: ½ hour   Cooking Time: ½ hour
Kcal/serve: 377
Soaking of jackfruit: 2 or 3 hours
Soaking of chana: Overnight

Ingredients:

- 1 unripe jackfruit, weighing about 3 lbs (1.5 kg)
- ½ cup horse gram, *left whole and unpeeled*
- 1 cup cooking oil
- 2 large potatoes, *cut into cubes*
- 1 teaspoon cummin seeds
- 5 sticks cinnamon, each 1 in (2.5 cm) long
- 5 cardamoms
- 2 large onions, *chopped*
- 1 tablespoon cummin seed powder
- 1 tablespoon pounded ginger
- ½ cup yogurt
- 4 bay leaves
- 2 tablespoons ghee
- 2 teaspoons garam masala powder

Method:

Select a medium-size jackfruit, unripe but sufficiently mature to have some seeds showing. Cut it in half, lengthwise, and then slice into 3 in (7 cm) pieces. Discard skin and straw-like fibres. Soak slices in water for 2-3 hours.

Pry out each jackfruit seed, including flesh surrounding it. Cut each seed into two and remove skin. Soak seeds in water for 2-3 hours.

Slice flesh into ½ in (1 cm) pieces; wash and soak together with seeds for 2-3 hours.

Wash horse gram after it has been soaked in water overnight; boil till half-cooked.

Heat oil in pan and fry potato cubes on medium heat till light brown. Remove and set aside.

In the same pan, fry cummin seeds, cinnamon, cardamoms and onions till light brown.

UNRIPE FRUIT

Put in jackfruit slices and halved seeds. Add salt, sugar and turmeric powder. Fry till jackfruit turns light brown and is half-cooked.

Add 1 cup water, chilli powder, cummin seed powder, ginger, yogurt, horse gram and bay leaves. Fry till all water is absorbed.

Put in fried potato cubes and add 3 cups water. Cover pan and simmer till gravy is thick and jackfruit and potato cubes are cooked.

Stir in ghee and garam masala just before removing from fire.

Serve Jackfruit Curry with bread or plain rice.

Note: It takes only about 15 minutes to cook this dish if you are using a pressure cooker.

UNRIPE PAPAYA CURRY (Bengal)

Serves: 6 *Preparation: 20 minutes Cooking Time: 30 minutes*
Kcal/serve: 247

Ingredients:

1	green unripe papaya, weighing about 1 lb (455g)
½	cup potato cubes
½	cup cooking oil
2	teaspoons salt
2	teaspoons turmeric powder
1	teaspoon cummin seeds
3	sticks cinnamon, each about 1 in (2.5 cm) long
4	cardamoms
4	bay leaves
1	onion, *chopped*
2	teaspoons chilli powder
2	teaspoons coriander seed powder
1	teaspoon sugar
½	cup green peas
1	teaspoon garam masala powder

Method:

Peel and cut papaya into small cubes; soak for 15 minutes, then wash and set aside.

Heat oil. When hot, fry potato cubes on medium heat. Add 1 teaspoon salt and 1 teaspoon turmeric powder, stirring frequently till potato cubes turn light brown. Remove and set aside.

In the same pan fry cummin seeds, cinnamon, cardamoms, bay leaves and chopped onion till slightly brown.

Add papaya cubes and fry with the remaining salt and turmeric powder till light brown.

Add 1 cup water, chilli powder, coriander powder and sugar. Fry till mixture turns dry.

Add the fried potato cubes and 2 cups water. Continue to cook on medium heat with pan covered.

When papaya and potato cubes are tender and well-cooked, add green peas and garam masala. Mix well and when gravy is thick, remove from fire.

MIXED FRUIT CHUTNEY (Bengal)

Serves: 6 Preparation: 10 minutes Cooking Time: 10 minutes Soaking of tamarind: 1 hour
Kcal/serve: 150

Ingredients:

- ½ cup tamarind pulp
- 3 teaspoons oil
- 4 dried red chillies
- 1 teaspoon mustard seeds
- 2 teaspoons shredded ginger
- 1 can fruit cocktail (You can use fresh cut fruit if you wish.)
- 1 cup sugar
- 2 tablespoons raisins
- 2 teaspoons salt

Method:

Soak tamarind in water for 1 hour, then squeeze to extract pulp.

Heat oil; fry dried red chillies and mustard seeds till they pop.

Add canned fruit (or fresh fruit), sugar, tamarind pulp, raisins and salt. Cook for a few minutes.

When gravy thickens, remove from fire and set aside to cool.

Serve with parathas or pooris.

Note: You can use fruits like pears, pineapples, grapes, prunes, dates and lychees.

Legumes and Lentils

LEGUMES AND LENTILS

Lentils, or dhall, form an essential aspect of the Indian diet – especially the Indian vegetarian diet – and are served at almost every meal. There are many varieties of dhall as well as different ways of preparing it, which makes it interesting despite its frequent appearance.

Dhall can be cooked dry or in liquid; soaked, ground and then formed into patties and fried.

As dhall is full of plant protein, it forms a nourishing part of the meal. It is also relatively inexpensive and easy to obtain. And its popularity among the Indians is clearly shown through this popular saying, "Come share my dhall" as a way of inviting guests to a home-cooked meal.

Legumes and Lentils and their Nutrient Contents

Calories	★ ★ ★ ★
Protein	★ ★ ★
Fat	★ ★
Calcium	★ ★
Iron	★ ★
Vitamin A	–
Vitamin B Complex	★
Vitamin C	–
Fibre	★ ★ ★ ★

None	–	Fair	★ ★ ★
Negligible	★	Good	★ ★ ★ ★
Some	★ ★	Very Good	★ ★ ★ ★ ★

LEGUMES AND LENTILS

GREEN SPLIT PEAS DHALL WITH SKIN (Punjab)

Serves: 6   *Preparation: 10 minutes   Cooking Time: 1 hour   Soaking of Dhall: Overnight*
Kcal/serve: 176

Ingredients:

- 1 cup green split peas (with skin)
- 2 teaspoons salt
- 2 teaspoons turmeric powder
- 1 teaspoon sugar
- 4 fresh green chillies
- 1 tablespoon cooking oil or ghee
- 1 teaspoon sweet cummin seeds
- 4 dried red chillies
- 2 teaspoons chopped ginger
- 1 large onion, *chopped*
- 5 cloves garlic, *chopped*
- 2 tomatoes, *sliced*

Method:

After the dhall has been soaked overnight, wash and boil with salt, turmeric powder, sugar and 1 pint (½ litre) water.

When dhall is tender, add fresh green chillies before removing from fire.

Heat oil (or ghee) in a pan. Fry sweet cummin seeds and dried chillies till light brown. Add ginger and onion; fry till slightly brown.

Add in tomatoes, garlic and the cooked dhall. Continue to cook for 10 minutes before removing from fire. (Mixture should be of medium consistency, so add a little water if it is too thick.)

Serve with plain rice or bread.

DHALL SAMBAR (Madras)

Serves: 6   Preparation: ½ hour   Cooking Time: 1 hour
Kcal/serve: 347

Ingredients:

- 2 teacups arahar dhall
- 2 teaspoons salt
- 2 teaspoons turmeric powder
- ½ cup sliced white radish
- ½ cup sliced eggplant
- ½ cup sliced okra
- ½ cup sliced drumstick
- ½ cup sliced carrot
- ½ cup sliced cauliflower

} cut into 1 inch (2.5 cm) slices

- 4 fresh green chillies
- 2 teaspoons chilli powder
- 2 teaspoons sugar
- 2 tomatoes, *halved*
- 2 tablespoons oil
- 4 dried red chillies
- A few curry leaves
- 1 teaspoon mustard seeds
- 2 teaspoons chopped ginger
- 2 onions, *chopped*
- 1 tablespoon tamarind juice

Method:

Wash dhall and then boil with salt and turmeric powder. Cook with saucepan covered.

When dhall is half-cooked, put in all the fresh vegetables except cauliflower, green chillies and tomatoes.

When vegetables are three-quarters cooked, add cauliflower, green chillies, chilli powder, sugar and tomatoes. Remove boiled mixture from fire when cauliflower is half-cooked.

Heat oil in a pan and fry dried red chillies, curry leaves and mustard seeds till they pop.

Add ginger and onions; fry till light brown. Add the cooked dhall and tamarind juice; leave to simmer for a few minutes before removing from fire.

Serve Dhall Sambar with plain rice.

Dhall Sambar

LEGUMES AND LENTILS

HORSE GRAM DHALL KOPTA CURRY (Bengal)

Serves: 6   Preparation: ½ hour   Cooking Time: ¾ hour   Soaking of Dhall: Overnight
Kcal/serve: 567

Ingredients:

- 1   cup horse gram, *soaked in water overnight*
- 1   cup oil
- 3   teaspoons chilli powder
- 2   onions, *pounded*
- 2   teaspoons pounded ginger
- 2   teaspoons plain flour
- 1   teaspoon cummin seeds
- 4   sticks cinnamon each approx. 1 inch (2.5 cm)
- 4   cardamoms
- 3   potatoes, *cubed*
- 2   teaspoons turmeric powder
- 1   teaspoon sugar
- 2   teaspoons salt
- 2   teaspoons cummin seed powder
- 4   bay leaves
- ½   cup beaten yogurt (or a few slices tomatoes)
- 1   teaspoon garam masala

Method:

Wash and grind horse gram dhall after it has been soaked overnight. (Add a little water if you are using a blender.)

Heat 1 tablespoon oil and on medium heat, fry the ground dhall with a little salt, 1 teaspoon chilli powder, the pounded onion, 1 teaspoon of the pounded ginger, and the plain flour till mixture becomes a thick paste.

Spread paste on a flat plate to cool. (When spread out, paste should be about 1 inch or 2.5 cm thick.) When mixture has cooled, cut into squares and set aside.
Heat oil again and fry the squares of dhall cake on medium heat till golden brown. Remove and set aside.
In the same pan, fry cummin seeds, cinnamon, cardamoms and potato cubes till light brown.
Add ½ cup water, the remaining 2 teaspoons chilli powder, turmeric powder, sugar, salt, cummin seed powder, bay leaves, the remaining teaspoon ginger, and yogurt. Fry mixture well.
Add 4 cups water and the fried dhall cakes. Continue to cook with pan covered.
When potatoes are tender, stir in garam masala and continue to simmer on low heat before removing from fire.

VEGETABLE DHALL (Bengal)

Serves: 6 *Preparation: ½ hour Cooking Time: 1 hour*
Kcal/serve: 336

Ingredients:

- 1 cup green split peas dhall (without skin)
- 2 teaspoons salt
- 2 teaspoons turmeric power
- 3 medium-size potatoes, *cubed*
- 10 French beans, cut into 2 in or 5 cm lengths
- 2 carrots, quartered and cut into 2 in or 5 cm lengths
- 3 or 4 cabbage leaves
- 2 teaspoons sugar
- 3 florets cauliflower, cut into bite-size pieces
- 4 fresh red chillies
- ¼ cup corn oil or ghee
- 3 medium-size tomatoes, *cut into halves*
- 4 dried red chillies
- 1 teaspoon small cummin seeds
- 2 teaspoons chopped ginger
- 2 medium-size onions, *peeled and chopped*
- ½ teacup fresh green peas
- 1 teaspoon garam masala
- 3 bay leaves
- 1 tablespoon chopped coriander leaves

Method:

Fry dhall on medium heat (without oil) till slightly brown; remove from fire and wash.

Boil washed dhall in a covered saucepan with salt and turmeric powder.

When dhall is three-quarters cooked, put in potatoes, French beans, carrots and cabbage.

When these vegetables are cooked, add sugar, cauliflower and fresh red chillies. Cook for 10 minutes more and then remove from fire.

Heat corn oil (or ghee) in a deep pan. Fry dried red chillies, cummin seeds, ginger and chopped onion till light brown.

Pour the cooked dhall and vegetable mixture into the pan. Add green peas, garam masala, bay leaves and the chopped coriander leaves, mixing thoroughly.

CHANA DHALL (Bengal)

Serves: 6 Preparation: 10 minutes Cooking Time: 30 minutes
Kcal/serve: 174
Soaking of dhall: 30 minutes

Ingredients:

- 1 cup chana (horse gram) dhall
- 2 teaspoons salt
- 1 teaspoon turmeric powder
- 1 tablespoon cooking oil or ghee
- 4 dried red chillies
- 2 teaspoons chopped ginger
- 1 teaspoon sugar
- 1 teaspoon cummin seeds
- 2 sticks cinnamon, each about 1 inch (2.5 cm long)
- 4 cardamoms
- 4 bay leaves
- 2 tablespoons grated or desiccated coconut
- 4 fresh green chillies

Method:

Soak dhall in cold water for 30 minutes. Wash and then boil with salt, turmeric powder and 1 pint (½ litre) water. Cover pan and cook on medium heat till dhall is tender.

Heat oil (or ghee). Fry dried red chillies on medium heat with sugar, ginger, cummin seeds, cinnamon, cardamoms and bay leaves till brown.

Add coconut and fry for 5 minutes. Add dhall; boil for another 5 minutes before removing from fire.

Note: Cooked mixture should be of porridge consistency. If using a pressure cooker, boil for 10 minutes and not longer so as not to break up the dhall.

LEGUMES AND LENTILS

MYSORE DHALL (Bengal)

This dhall has a thin consistency and can be eaten on its own like a soup, or with rice.

Serves: 6   *Preparation: 10 minutes   Cooking Time: 1 hour*
            Kcal/serve: 160

Ingredients:

- 1 cup mysore dhall (red lentils)
- 1 tablespoon oil or ghee
- 1 teaspoon black cummin seeds
- 4 dried red chillies
- 1 large onion, *chopped*
- 3 teaspoons salt
- 1 teaspoon turmeric powder
- 4 fresh green chillies
- 10 shallots, *peeled but left whole*
- A few coriander leaves, *chopped*

Method:

Soak the lentils in cold water for 10 minutes; wash, drain and set aside.

Heat oil (or ghee) in saucepan and fry black cummin seeds and dried chillies till light brown. Add chopped onion and fry till light brown.

Add dhall, salt and turmeric powder; fry about 10 minutes or till dhall turns slightly brown. Then add 1 pint (½ litre) water. Continue to cook with pan covered.

When dhall is cooked, remove from fire. Mash dhall to a smooth paste, using an egg-beater or a big spoon.

Put the mashed dhall mixture back in the saucepan. Add fresh green chillies and shallots and continue to cook for 10 minutes on medium heat.

Add chopped coriander leaves just before removing from fire. (Mixture should be of porridge consistency, so add more water if necessary.)

Serve with plain rice or bread.

LEGUMES AND LENTILS

Savouries

SAVOURIES

ALU AND MATAR SAMOSA (Punjab)

Samosas are among the most popular Indian savouries. A lightly-fried batter enclosing deliciously prepared vegetables makes it easy to understand why this is so.

Serves: 6   **Preparation: 1 hour**   **Cooking Time: 5 minutes**
Kcal/serve: 340

Ingredients:

- 2 medium-size potatoes, *cut into cubes*
- 2 cups cooking oil
- 2 teaspoons salt
- 1 large onion, *chopped*
- 2 teaspoons shredded ginger
- 2 teaspoons chilli powder
- 1 teaspoon sugar
- 1 tablespoon raisins
- 2 teaspoons sweet cummin seed powder, *fried*
- ½ cup green peas
- 3 cups plain flour
- 1 teaspoon baking powder

Method:

Filling:

Wash and fry potato cubes in 2 tablespoons oil. Add a little salt, onion and ginger; fry till brown.

Add chilli powder, sugar and 1 cup water. Add raisins, cummin seed powder and green peas. Fry till mixture turns dry.

Flour Mixture:

Sift flour, the remaining salt, and baking powder. Rub in 3 tablespoons oil and add water gradually till dough turns smooth and elastic. Form small balls with dough.

Roll out each ball onto a lightly floured board and shape it like a flat saucer. Cut each shape in half, so that each becomes a semi-circle.

Put 1 teaspoon of filling on one half, brush edges with water and fold over to cover filling. Press edges firmly together again to form a triangle-shaped samosa. Repeat with remaining balls.

Heat oil for deep-frying. When hot, turn heat to low and fry a few samosas at a time till golden brown. Remove and drain excess oil.

SAVOURIES

Cabbage Roll

SAVOURIES

CABBAGE ROLL (Bengal)

Serves: 6　　Preparation: 15 minutes　　Cooking Time: 10 minutes
　　　　　　Kcal/serve: 182

Ingredients:

- 1　large cabbage
- ½　cup oil
- 2　teaspoons chopped ginger
- 1　large onion, *chopped*
- 2　potatoes, *cut into cubes*
- ½　cup shredded cabbage
- 2　carrots, *peeled and shredded*
- 4　florets cauliflower, *cut into cubes*
- 2　teaspoons salt
- 1　teaspoon sugar
- 1　tablespoon chilli powder
- 1　teaspoon garam masala powder
- 2　teaspoons fried cummin seed powder
- ½　cup green peas
- 1　cup self-raising flour

Method:

Separate leaves of cabbage and boil in salted water till half-cooked. Drain off water and set aside cabbage leaves to cool and dry.

Heat oil and fry ginger and onion on medium heat till light brown. Add potato cubes and shredded cabbage and carrot.

When potato cubes turn a golden brown, add cauliflower cubes, 1 teaspoon salt, sugar, chilli powder and 1 cup water. Continue to cook with pan covered.

When vegetables are cooked, add garam masala, fried cummin seed powder and green peas. Fry for a short while and then remove from heat.

Mix the flour and the remaining teaspoon salt with sufficient water to form a soft batter.

Take one cabbage leaf and lay it flat on a plate or chopping board. Place some cooked vegetable mixture in the centre of leaf. Roll leaf to cover mixture and then secure both edges with toothpicks. Repeat with remaining cabbage leaves.

Heat enough oil for deep-frying.

Dip cabbage rolls in the prepared batter and then fry on medium heat till light brown. Drain off excess oil and place cabbage rolls on absorbent paper to cool.

SAVOURIES

CHEESE PAKURA (Sindhi)

Pakuras are crisp vegetable fritters. This recipe, made with cheese, is a variation on that theme. Cheese Pakuras are best eaten as soon as they are cooked.

Serves: 6   Preparation: 20 minutes   Cooking Time: 10 minutes
Kcal/serve: 198

Ingredients:

- 1 cup plain flour
- 2 teaspoons salt
- 1 teaspoon sugar
- 4 fresh green chillies
- 1 onion, *chopped*
- 1 teaspoon baking powder
- 1 egg, *beaten*
- A few coriander leaves, *chopped*
- 1 cup cooking oil

Method:

Mix flour with salt, sugar, chillies, chopped onion, baking powder, egg, and a little water to make a thick batter. Add grated cheese and coriander leaves.

Heat oil for deep-frying. When oil is hot, drop teaspoonfuls of the batter into pan. Fry till light brown and remove, draining excess oil. Repeat with the remaining batter.

Serve Cheese Pakura hot with chutney.

SAVOURIES

RADISH PAKURA (Sindhi)

Serves: 6   Preparation: 15 minutes   Cooking Time: 10 minutes
Kcal/serve: 314

Ingredients:

- 1 cup grated radish
- ½ cup horse gram dhall flour
- ½ cup self-raising flour
- 2 teaspoons salt
- 1 teaspoon baking powder
- 2 teaspoons chilli powder
- 1 teaspoon small cummin seeds
- 1 cup oil

Method:

Wash grated radish. Add a pinch of salt, squeeze and discard juice.

Mix horse gram dhall flour and self-raising flour with salt, baking powder, chilli powder and cummin seeds.

Add water to mixture to form a very thick batter. Add grated radish and mix well. Form round, flat balls with mixture.

Heat oil for deep-frying. When oil is hot, fry pakura till golden brown and crisp. Remove and drain.

Serve Radish Pakura with sauce.

SAVOURIES

STUFFED FRIED SANDWICH (Bengal)

Serves: 6   *Preparation: 10 minutes   Cooking Time: 5 minutes*
              Kcal/serve: 398

Ingredients:

- ½ cup cooking oil
- 2 onions, *chopped*
- 2 teaspoons shredded ginger
- 3 large potatoes, *boiled and mashed*
- 1 teaspoon salt
- 1 teaspoon sugar
- 2 teaspoons chilli powder
- 1 tablespoon cashewnuts, *fried and pounded*
- 2 teaspoons chopped mint leaves
- 10 slices bread, *cut very thinly*
- 3 teaspoons corn flour, *mixed with a little water to form a paste*

Method:

Heat 2 tablespoons oil till smoking. Fry onion and ginger till golden brown.

Add mashed potato, salt, sugar and chilli powder; fry thoroughly. Just before removing from fire, add ground cashewnut and chopped mint leaves.

Spread mixture over slices of bread. Fold each slice over and "seal" edges with the corn flour paste.

Heat oil for deep-frying. Fry a few slices of bread at a time till golden brown. Drain off excess oil and remove from heat.

Eat Stuffed Sandwich plain or with sauce or chutney.

Thosai and Thosai Chutney

SAVOURIES

THOSAI OR SHALLOW FRIED PANCAKE (South India)

Serves: 6 *Preparation: 15 minutes Cooking Time: 5 minutes*
Kcal/serve: 296
Soaking of dhall and rice: 6 hours

Ingredients:

- 1 cup rice
- ½ cup black split peas (urhad dhall)
- 2 teaspoons salt
- 2 teaspoons sugar
- 2 teaspoons baking powder
- 1 tablespoon beaten yogurt
- 2 onions, *chopped*
- 4 fresh green chillies, *chopped*
- ¼ cup cooking oil

Method:

Soak rice and dhall separately for 6 hours. After they have been soaked, wash and grind each separately into a smooth and fine paste.

Mix both the pastes in a big bowl. Add salt, sugar, baking powder, yogurt and enough water to make a light batter. Beat mixture well and cover for 5-6 hours.

After 5-6 hours, batter is ready for frying. Add chopped onions and chillies.

Heat a heavy pan on medium heat; grease pan with oil.

Scoop a ladleful of batter and spread it all over pan with a wooden spoon. Cook for 2 minutes with pan covered; turn over batter and cook for another 2 minutes.

Remove thosai and repeat with remaining batter.

Serve Thosai with Thosai Chutney.

Note: Cooked vegetables or some dry curry can be placed in the centre of uncooked thosais and folded over to make stuffed thosais.

THOSAI CHUTNEY (South India)

Serves: 6 Preparation: 10 minutes Cooking Time: 5 minutes
Kcal/serve: 75

Ingredients:

- 1 cup grated coconut
- 4 fresh green chillies
- 1 teaspoon chopped ginger
- 2 teaspoons salt
- 2 small onions, *chopped*
- 3 teaspoons oil
- 1 teaspoon mustard seeds
- 8 curry leaves
- 3 teaspoons sugar
- 1 tablespoon tamarind pulp or 1 tablespoon lemon juice

Method:

Grind coconut with chillies, ginger, salt and onions to form a smooth paste.

Heat oil; fry mustard seeds and curry leaves for a few minutes.

Add in the ground coconut mixture, sugar and tamarind pulp (or lemon juice). Stir for a few minutes and then remove from fire. (If mixture is too thick, add a little water.)

Serve with hot thosai.

SAVOURIES

Stuffed Tomato and Stuffed Capsicum

SAVOURIES

STUFFED TOMATO (Bengal)

Serves: 8   Preparation: 10 minutes   Cooking Time: 5 minutes
Kcal/serve: 90

Ingredients:

- 8 large red tomatoes
- 2 teaspoons sugar
- ¼ cup thick yogurt
- 2 teaspoons chat masala or roasted cummin seed powder
- ¼ cup grated cheese
- 2 teaspoons lemon juice
- 1 cup very finely sliced pineapple
- 1 cup grated cucumber
- ½ cup green peas
- 3 fresh green chillies, *chopped*
- 2 teaspoons salt

Method:

Wash tomatoes with hot water and slice off about ¼ in (0.5 cm) from top. Using a small, sharp knife, hollow tomatoes by cutting away the centres and removing pulp.

Mix pulp with sugar, yogurt, chat masala (or roasted cuumin seed powder), cheese and lemon juice.

Stuff each hollowed-out tomato with the mixture and cover with a sliced-off end.

Keep in refrigerator to cool till ready to serve.

For accompanying salad, mix pineapple, cucumber, green peas and green chillies with salt.

Note: You can also bake the stuffed tomatoes if you prefer. Set oven at 400° F and bake for 5 minutes.

SAVOURIES

STUFFED CAPSICUM (Sindhi)

Serves: 8   *Preparation: 10 minutes*   *Cooking Time: 10 minutes*
Kcal/serve: 300

Ingredients:

8	capsicums
½	cup oil
2	onions, *chopped*
2	medium-size potatoes
1	medium-size carrot
3	florets cauliflower

cut into very small cubes (applies to potatoes, carrot, cauliflower)

2	teaspoons salt
2	teaspoons sugar
2	teaspoons chilli powder
1	teaspoon garam masala
1	tablespoon cashewnut powder, *fried*

Method:

Wash capsicums and slice off about ¼ inch (0.5 cm) from top. Set aside.

Using a small, sharp knife, hollow capsicums by cutting away centres.

Heat oil on medium heat and fry onions till brown. Add potato, carrot and cauliflower cubes together with salt, sugar, chilli powder and a little water. Cover pan and cook till potatoes and carrots are done.

Stir in garam masala and fried cashewnut powder; mix thoroughly. When mixture turns dry, remove from heat.

Fill hollowed-out capsicums with cooked vegetable mixture. Cover with sliced capsicum ends.

Bake capsicums at 400° F for about 10 minutes, then remove from oven.

DAHI BARHE (Rajstan)

Serves: 10 Preparation: ½ hour   Cooking Time: 1 hour
Kcal/serve: 344
Soaking of Dhall: Overnight

Ingredients:

1½ cups black split dhall (unhusked urhad dhall)
3   teaspoons salt
2   teaspoons asafoetida
2   cups corn oil
4   cups thick yogurt
3   teaspoons chilli powder
1   cup sugar
½   cup thick tamarind pulp
2   teaspoons cummin seed powder, *fried*
    A few coriander leaves

Method:

Soak the dhall overnight in cold water. After dhall has been soaked, wash and drain. Grind with 1 teaspoon salt, and asafoetida. Use a long wooden spoon to beat and mix well.

Form flat, round balls with the mixture, leaving a hollow in the centre of each ball.

Heat oil till smoking. Fry the balls, a few at a time, till they turn light brown on both sides. Remove and set aside to cool.

Beat 1 cup yogurt with 3 cups warm water. Add 1 teaspoon salt and 1 teaspoon chilli powder. Soak the fried dhall cakes in the yogurt mixture.

Beat the remaining 3 cups yogurt with ½ cup sugar and ½ teaspoon salt.

Mix the tamarind pulp with the remaining sugar, ½ teaspoon salt and the remaining teaspoon chilli powder.

Arrange the cooled dhall cakes onto a shallow dish. Pour the yogurt mixture on top of the cakes and the tamarind mixture on the sides.

Sprinkle all the cakes with cummin seed powder and garnish with the coriander leaves.

Pickles and Chutneys

MANGO CHUTNEY (Bengal)

Serves: 6   *Preparation: 30 minutes   Cooking Time: 20 minutes*
            Kcal/serve: 148

Ingredients:

- 10 mangoes
- 1 tablespoon oil
- 5 dried red chillies
- 1 teaspoon mustard seeds
- 2 teaspoon chopped ginger
- 2 tablespoons raisins
- 2 teaspoons salt
- 2 teaspoons mustard seed powder
- 1 teaspoon turmeric powder
- 2 cups sugar
- 2 teaspoons ground sweet cummin seeds, *roasted*

Method:

Peel and cut each mango into 4. Remove seeds, wash and set aside.

Heat oil and fry dried chillies, mustard seeds, chopped ginger and raisins on medium heat till light brown.

Add mango, salt, mustard seed powder, turmeric powder and sugar. Stir till sugar turns brown and mango turns soft. Stir in sweet cummin seeds before removing from fire.

Cool and store in glass jar.

Note: Chutney can be stored for one month in the refrigerator and up to a year in the freezer.

PAPAYA CHUTNEY (Bengal)

Serves: 6   Preparation: 10 minutes   Cooking Time: 30 minutes
Kcal/serve: 180

Ingredients:

- 2 green papayas
- 1 cup sugar
- 2 teaspoons chopped ginger
- 2 teaspoons salt
- 1 tablespoon unpeeled almonds, *chopped*
- 2 lemons, *squeezed for juice*
- 4 fresh red or green chillies, *chopped*

Method:

Peel and cut papayas into thin strips about 1 inch (3cm) long. Wash and boil till half-cooked; drain and discard liquid.

Boil sugar with 4 cups water till it thickens slightly.

Add chopped ginger, salt, almonds and boiled papaya strips. Cook till papaya turns soft. Continue to simmer, add lemon juice and sliced chillies; mix well.

Serve Papaya Chutney cool.

SWEET AND SOUR MANGO CHUTNEY (Bengal)

Serves: 6   Preparation: 10 minutes   Cooking Time: 10 minutes
Kcal/serve: 398

Ingredients:

- 10 mangoes
- 2 cups sugar
- 2 teaspoons chilli powder
- 2 teaspoons chopped ginger
- 3 teaspoons chopped onions
- 2 teaspoons salt
- 2 teaspoons mustard powder

Method:

Peel, wash and grate mangoes.

Boil sugar with 2 cups water. Add chilli powder, chopped ginger, onions and salt; cook till mixture turns to a soft and thick syrup.

Stir in grated mango and mustard powder. Cook till mango turns soft and then remove from fire.

Cool before storing in a glass jar.

Note: If you want Sweet and Sour Mango Chutney to keep for a few months, add ½ cup vinegar when boiling the sugar.

EGGPLANT PICKLE (Maharastra)

Serves: 6   Preparation: 10 minutes   Cooking Time: 20 minutes
Kcal/serve: 345

Ingredients:

- 5   eggplants
- ½   cup oil
- 4   cloves garlic, *ground*
- 2   teaspoons chopped ginger
- 2   teaspoons salt
- 2   teaspoons chilli powder
- 1   cup sugar
- ½   cup vinegar
- 2   teaspoons ground sweet cummin seeds, *roasted*

Method:

Cut each eggplant in half and slice into 3 inch (8 cm) lengths; wash and drain.

Heat oil; fry garlic and chopped ginger on medium heat for a few minutes.

Add eggplant, salt and chilli powder. When eggplant is half-cooked, add sugar and vinegar; continue cooking till eggplant turns soft.

Stir in roasted sweet cummin seeds just before removing from fire.

Cool before storing in a glass jar.

MANGO PICKLE (Uttar Pradesh)

Serves: 6   *Preparation: 20 minutes   Cooking Time: 10 minutes*
Kcal/serve: 240
Drying of mangoes: 2-3 days   Seasoning: 2-3 weeks

Ingredients:

- 10 mangoes
- 3 teaspoons salt
- 2 teaspoons turmeric powder
- 2 teaspoons chilli powder
- 3 cups olive oil or mustard oil, *heated*
- 2 teaspoons sweet cummin seeds, *roasted*
- 2 teaspoons black cummin seeds, *roasted*
- 2 teaspoons fenugreek, *roasted*
- 6 fresh red chillies

Method:

Cut unpeeled mangoes into 4; remove seeds.

Add salt, turmeric powder and chilli powder. Leave the seasoned mangoes in the sun for 2 days.

Put dried mangoes in a glass jar. Pour in the oil and add roasted sweet cummin seeds, black cummin seeds and fenugreek, and fresh chillies. Stir well and season for a further 2-3 weeks.

Note: Mango Pickle keeps for up to a year when stored in a cool place.

GREEN LIME PICKLE (South India)

Serves: 6   *Preparation: 20 minutes   Cooking Time: 20 minutes*
Kcal/serve: 165

Ingredients:

- 10 green limes
- 3 teaspoons salt
- 1 teaspoon turmeric powder
- 1 teaspoon fenugreek, *fried*
- 5 limes, squeezed for juice
- 2 teaspoons sweet cummin seeds, *fried*
- 2 teaspoons black cummin seeds, *fried*
- 6 fresh red chillies

PICKLES AND CHUTNEYS

Method:

Wash green limes in boiling water and then cut them in halves; squeeze and set aside juice.

Mix the halved limes with salt and turmeric powder; leave in the sun for 2-3 days and then put them in a glass jar.

Add the lime juice, fenugreek, sweet cummin seeds and black cummin seeds, and fresh chillies. Shake jar to mix all the ingredients well.

Leave Lime Pickle covered in the jar for 2-3 weeks, after which time it should be soft and well-seasoned.

Note: Lime Pickle keeps for up to one year when stored in a cool place.

TAMARIND CHUTNEY (North India)

Serves: 8   Preparation: 20 minutes   Cooking Time: 20 minutes   Soaking of Tamarind: 2 hours
Kcal/serve: 28

Ingredients:

½	cup dried tamarind
2	cups water
	Sugar and salt to taste
2	teaspoons chilli powder
2	teaspoons mustard seed powder
1	teaspoon sweet cummin seed powder, *roasted*

Method:

Soak tamarind in water for 2 hours.

Mix tamarind, using fingers, and then pass through strainer to collect the liquid pulp in a bowl. (Press tamarind with a wooden spoon so that you get as much pulp as possible.)

To the pulp, add salt, sugar and chilli powder. Mix thoroughly and then fry for 20 minutes before removing from fire.

To the cooked mixture, add mustard seed powder and cummin seed powder. Mix well before removing from fire to cool. (Mixture must be of a thick consistency.)

Note: Tamarind Chutney keeps for 1 year in the refrigerator.

PICKLES AND CHUTNEYS

RAITA

Raita is the name given to yogurt-based side dishes. Cool raitas enhance spicy food and because fresh ingredients are used, they look good at the table. Featured here are some variations of the Raita.

RAITA POTATO

Serves: 6   *Preparation: 10 minutes   Cooking Time: 20 minutes*
             Kcal/serve: 98

Ingredients:

2	large potatoes
2	cups beaten yogurt
3	teaspoons sugar
2	teaspoons salt
2	teaspoons small cummin seed powder, *roasted*
2	fresh red or green chillies, *sliced finely*
1	medium-size onion, *chopped very finely*
1	tablespoon chopped coriander leaves

} basic Raita ingredients

Method:

Boil potatoes in their jackets. When they have cooled, peel and cut into small pieces.

Mix beaten yogurt with the potato pieces.

Add all the rest of the ingredients, sprinkling the coriander leaves on top.

Serve Raita Potato cool.

PICKLES AND CHUTNEYS

RAITA BANANA

Slice 4 yellow ripe bananas and add Raita ingredients.

RAITA MARROW

Par-boil 1 marrow. When it has cooled, peel, grate and then squeeze to discard juice. Large seeds should also be discarded. Add Raita ingredients, with a little lemon juice if preferred.

RAITA MINT AND ONION

Instead of potatoes, add mint leaves and onions. Use 4 medium-size onions, sliced finely, and 3 tablespoons coarsely-chopped mint leaves. You can also add 2 tablespoons tamarind pulp.

RAITA CUCUMBER

Grate 1 large cucumber, unpeeled, and add Raita ingredients.

Desserts and Sweet Drinks

DESSERTS AND SWEET DRINKS

ROSSO NOBONI (Bengal)

Serves: 6   *Preparation: 30 minutes   Cooking Time: 30 minutes*
           Kcal/serve: 465

Ingredients:

1	cup thick milk cream
2	tablespoons white vinegar
6	cups cold water
3	teaspoons melted ghee
1	teaspoon ground semolina
1	teaspoon plain flour
½	teaspoon cardamom powder
	A few pieces of rock sugar
2	cups sugar
5	cups water

Method:

Mix vinegar with 6 cups cold water.

Heat thick milk cream. When hot, pour in the vinegar and stir slowly till milk curdles. Remove from fire and set aside for 10 minutes.

Strain curdled milk through fine muslin, holding it under a running tap to wash. Tie ends of cloth to form a 'bag' and leave to hang till all liquid is drained. The semi-solid milk is now known as panir.

Mix panir with melted ghee, semolina powder, plain flour and cardamom powder; knead well. Divide mixture into small balls.

Place a piece of rock sugar in the centre of each ball and then close up.

For syrup, boil 5 cups water with the sugar. When sugar dissolves, drop rock sugar-filled panir balls into the hot syrup. Panir balls are cooked when they sink to the bottom of the syrup.

Keep the balls simmering in the syrup on medium heat, stirring frequently so that syrup soaks in thoroughly.

When syrup becomes too thick, add more water. (Syrup should be thin and not too sweet.)

After a few minutes, remove from fire and leave to cool before serving.

DESSERTS AND SWEET DRINKS

LASSI OR BUTTER MILK SHERBET (North India)

Serves: 6   Preparation: 15 minutes
            Kcal/serve: 191

Ingredients:

4   cups yogurt
4   cups cold water
½   cup sugar
2   teaspoons salt
2   tablespoons lemon juice

Method:

Mix yogurt with cold water, sugar and salt. Beat well, using an egg beater or a blender. (This mixture is known as buttermilk.)

Add lemon juice into the buttermilk and cool in refrigerator.

Add ice cubes just before serving.

Note: If you wish, you may add a drop of rose water for a distinctive taste.

THANDAI OR ALMOND SHERBET (Punjab)

Almonds are rich in protein and good food value, so this drink is ideal in hot weather when you feel like consuming more liquids than solids.

Serves: 6   Preparation: 30 minutes   Kcal/serve: 190   Soaking of almonds: 2 hours

Ingredients:

40   almonds
20   raisins, *pounded*
5   glasses cold or boiled milk
      Sugar to taste
      A few drops essence of any flavour

DESSERTS AND SWEET DRINKS

Method:

Soak almonds in hot water for about 2 hours. Peel and grind almonds in a blender to form a smooth paste.

Mix the pounded raisins with the almond paste. Add milk, and sugar to taste. Cool in refrigerator.

Serve in tall glasses and add a little essence in each.

BESHAN LADDU (Gujerat)

Serves: 6 *Preparation Time: 10 minutes* *Cooking Time: 30 minutes*
Kcal/serve: 234

Ingredients:

- 1 cup horsegram dhall flour (beshan)
- ¼ cup melted ghee
- 1 teaspoon black peppercorns, *crushed*
- 1 teaspoon cardamom powder
- 2 teaspoons chopped pistachios
- ½ cup castor sugar
  Unsweetened milk, optional

Method:

Sift dhall flour. Heat pan and stir-fry flour and melted ghee on low heat till golden-brown.

Add pepper, cardamom and chopped pistachios; mix thoroughly. Remove from heat.

While mixture is still hot, rub in the castor sugar and immediately roll into small balls.

Note: Beshan Laddu can be kept in the refrigerator for as long as 2 weeks.

DESSERTS AND SWEET DRINKS

ORANGE KULFI (Bengal)

Kulfi, or Indian-style ice-cream, is less creamy than Western-style ice-cream since it contains no egg. The traditional way of setting it is by packing it tightly into tin cones. If these are unavailable, you can use cup-shaped tupperware containers.

Serves: 6   *Preparation Time: 20 minutes   Kcal/serve: 230*

Ingredients:

- ½ cup sugar
- 1 tablespoon gelatine
- 2 cups evaporated milk, *chilled for about two days*
- 1 cup whipped cream
- 1 cup sweetened orange juice
  A few drops orange food colouring
- 2 drops orange flavour

Method:

Boil sugar and gelatine with 2 cups water. When sugar dissolves, remove from heat and set aside to cool.

Beat milk and whipped cream till frothy.

Add orange juice, colouring and flavour; beat to mix thoroughly.

Place kulfi mixture in a bowl and chill in the freezer.

When kulfi is half-set, remove and beat it again. Pour beaten kulfi into containers; place in refrigerator to freeze.

Remove kulfi from containers just before serving.

Note: Kulfi can be served plain or with fruit, and nuts like pistachio.

WATERMELON SHERBET (Bengal)

Serves: 6   *Preparation: 15 minutes*
  Kcal/serve: 258

Ingredients:

- 3 watermelons
- 1 cup sugar
  A pinch of salt
- 3 cups cold water
- 1 tablespoon lemon juice

DESSERTS AND SWEET DRINKS

Method:

Scoop out the pulp from the watermelons. Remove seeds and mash pulp in a bowl. (Use a blender if possible.)

Add sugar and salt to taste, then add cold water to dilute pulp mixture. Chill in refrigerator.

Serve in tall glasses with ice cubes and a little lemon juice to taste. Decorate with a slice of lemon or a sprig of mint.

PANIR KHEER (Bengal)

Serves: 6   Preparation Time: ½ hour   Cooking Time: ½ hour
Kcal/serve: 450

Ingredients:

1   cup panir
10 cups fresh milk
1   cup sugar
10 almonds, *peeled and chopped*
10 pistachios, *peeled and chopped*
40 raisins
2   teaspoons cardamom powder
2   pistachio nuts, *peeled and chopped*

Method:

Tie panir in a muslin bag and leave it for about 3 hours till it hardens; remove and cut into small cubes.

Boil milk and sugar on medium heat. Stir constantly to prevent burning.

When milk is quite thick, add almonds, pistachio, raisins and the panir cubes. Continue to cook on very low heat, stirring constantly.

When mixture turns creamy and thick, remove from heat. Stir in cardamom powder and mix well.

Serve Panir Kheer when it has completly cooled.

DESSERTS AND SWEET DRINKS

In-Guide
A few minutes spent choosing the freshest vegetables available at the market pays handsome dividends in taste and nutrition. In this chart are hints on how to select the best produce, how to keep them fresh, and the basic steps you need to prepare them for cooking.

Vegetable	Choosing	Storing	Preparing
BANANAS, Unripe	Choose bright green bananas that are blemish-free.	Wrap unwashed bananas in newspaper and refrigerate for up to one week.	Peel and cut bananas lengthwise into 4 quarters; slice each quarter into 2 inch (5 cm) pieces.
BEAN SPROUTS	Select bean sprouts that are crisp with beans attached.	Wrap unwashed sprouts in newspaper and refrigerate for up to four days.	Rinse and discard any beans that are attached. Pluck off tails if you prefer.
FRENCH BEANS	Choose small crisp beans that are bright green and blemish-free.	Wrap unwashed beans in newspaper and refrigerate for up to two weeks.	Rinse beans; snap off and discard ends. Cut beans crosswise or in diagonal slices.
LONG BEANS	Choose thin beans that are dark green and blemish-free.	Wrap unwashed beans in newspaper and refrigerate for up to two weeks.	Rinse beans and cut ends off. Slice beans between $1/4$ and $1½$ inches (1-3 cm) apart.
BITTER GOURD	Select small bitter gourds that are firm and brightly-coloured.	Wrap unwashed bitter gourd in newspaper and keep refrigerated for up to two weeks.	Rinse bitter gourd; cut and discard stem. Slice thinly if frying and about 1 inch (2.5 cm) long and $1/2$ inch (1.5 cm) thick if cooking in a curry.
CABBAGE	Choose firm heads that feel heavy for their size. Outer leaves should look fresh, have a good, healthy colour and be blemish-free.	Wrap unwashed cabbage in newspaper and keep refrigerated for up to one week.	Discard leaves that are wilted. Rinse cabbage, cut in half lengthwise, and remove core. Shred leaves.
CHINESE CABBAGE	Look for fresh, crisp leaves that are blemish-free.	Wrap unwashed cabbage in newspaper and keep refrigerated for up to four days.	Discard leaves that are wilted. Rinse cabbage, cut off base and discard. Slice cabbage lengthwise and then crosswise.

CAULIFLOWER	Choose firm, creamy-white heads that are pressed tightly together. A yellow tinge and spreading florets indicate over-maturity.	Wrap unwashed cauliflower in newspaper and refrigerate for up to one week.	vegetable peeler or a small, sharp knife. Rinse and then dice or shred.
CUCUMBER	Choose firm, dark green cucumbers that are well-shaped and slender. Soft, yellowing cucumbers are over-mature.	Refrigerate whole and unwrapped for up to one week.	Slice about 1 cm (½ inch) off each end. Use cut-off ends to rub into the part of cucumber that has been cut; this will bring out the sticky 'sap' which is bitter. Once this is done, slice off just a bit of the ends again. You can choose to leave the skin on or have it peeled. Chop or slice cucumber.
DRUMSTICK	Look for dark green drumsticks which are not too thick and fleshy.	Wrap unwashed drumsticks in newspaper and refrigerate for up to two weeks.	Peel skin off and remove fibrous hairs. Cut drumstick in 1 inch (2.5 cm) slices.
EGGPLANT, also known as brinjal	Look for firm, shiny, deep purple eggplants with bright green stems. A dull colour and rust-coloured spots are a sign of old age.	Wrap unwashed eggplants in newspaper and refrigerate for up to one week.	Cut and discard stem. Slice eggplants about 1 inch (2.5 cm) apart.
GARLIC	Select firm, dry bulbs with tightly-closed cloves and smooth skins. Avoid bulbs with sprouting green shoots.	Store garlic, unwrapped, in a cool, dry and dark place with good ventilation for up to two months.	Wash and peel off skin before pounding or chopping.
HERBS	Choose herbs with a fresh green colour all over.	Wrap unwashed herbs in newspaper.	Wash and then slice finely or chop.

Vegetable	Choosing	Storing	Preparing
JACKFRUIT, Unripe	The skin should be firm and light green in colour.	Store jackfruit, uncut, in a cool, dry and dark place with good ventilation for up to four days.	Cut jackfruit into half, lengthwise. Then cut up each half into 3 inch (7 cm) slices. Discard the skin and the straw-like fibres inside. Cut each seed into half and remove outer casing.
LETTUCE	Select lettuce with crisp, fresh-looking leaves without spots or signs of decay.	Store dry lettuce in an air-tight plastic container and refrigerate for up to two weeks.	Lettuce leaves are usually used to decorate dishes or as a base for vegetable fillings. Snap off each leaf separately; wash and dry.
OKRA	Select pods that are firm and bend easily. They should be of a deep green colour.	Wrap unwashed okra in newspaper and refrigerate for up to 3 days.	Cut and discard stem ends. Rinse and slice okra diagonally about 1/4 inch apart.
ONIONS AND SHALLOTS	Select compact, dry bulbs with brittle skin that comes off easily. Avoid those with green shoots and dark spots.	Keep onions, whole and unwrapped, in a cool, dry and dark place with good ventilation for up to 2 months.	Cut off and discard stem and fibrous root ends. Peel skin. Cut onions into halves and then chop or pound.
PAPAYA, Unripe	Select papaya which is dark green on the outside. The inside of the fruit should be a pale white.	Wrap papaya in newspaper and refrigerate for up to two weeks.	Cut and discard stem. Peel papaya and cut in thin slices.
GREEN PEAS	Choose tiny, plump, bright green pods that are firm and crisp.	Wrap unwashed pods in newspaper and refrigerate for up to three days.	Split open pods with a knife, if necessary, to remove peas. This process is called shelling.
SNOW PEAS	Select crisp, firm, bright green pods.	Wrap unwashed pods in newspaper and refrigerate for up to three days.	Break off both ends and discard. Remove fibrous hairs.

PEPPERS	Choose peppers that are [brightly] coloured, firm and thick-walled; avoid those with soft spots.	Wrap unwashed peppers in newspaper and refrigerate for up to five days.	Discard stem. Rinse and cut peppers in half, lengthwise. Remove seeds and pith and then slice, dice or cut into julienne strips.
POTATOES	Select firm potatoes. Avoid those with sprouting 'eyes', soft black spots and green patches.	Store potatoes, unwrapped, in a cool, dry and dark place with good ventilation for up to two months.	Rinse and peel potatoes. Cut into quarters, cubes, or round slices. To prevent potatoes from getting discoloured, submerge them in a bowl of cold water immediately after removing skin.
PUMPKIN	Choose pumpkins that have hard, thick walls and feel heavy for their size. When cut, the 'meat' should be fleshy and have a bright orange colour.	Wrap cut pieces in newspaper and refrigerate for up to five days.	Rinse and cut pumpkin in half, lengthwise; peel and cut into cubes. Remove and discard seeds and fibrous bits.
RADISH	Select heavy radishes that are smooth and firm.	Wrap unwashed radishes in newspaper and refrigerate for up to two weeks.	Discard ends and scrape skin off; cut into slices or cubes.
SPINACH	Look out for crisp, tender, dark green leaves.	Rinse; keep bunches of spinach, wrapped in a kitchen towel, in a plastic bag. Refrigerate for up to three days.	Shred into pieces.
TOMATOES	Tomatoes should be well-formed, with a bright healthy colour and smooth skins. They should feel firm to the touch and not hard.	Wrap unwashed tomatoes in newspaper and refrigerate for up to four days.	Cut off ends and then slice, chop or cut into wedges as required.
TURNIP	Choose turnips that have smooth skins and are heavy for their size.	Wrap unwashed turnips in newspaper and refrigerate for up to one week.	Rinse, peel and then dice, slice, quarter or cut into julienne strips.